Inspire.

DEVOTIONS FOR BUSY YOUNGSTERS

Psalm 139

Finding identity

BY

PAUL MARTIN

Illustrations by Paul Martin.

Other books by this author:
Inspire. Devotions for busy youngsters. Psalm 34 - A recipe for faith.
LEADERS GUIDE Inspire. Devotions for busy youngsters. Psalm 34 .
Inspire. A resource for busy youth workers. Volumes 1 & 2.

Cover design adapted from line drawings by Amy Walters
www.amywaltersart.com

Artwork for cover adapted and modified from an original line drawing by
Amy Walters. Permission is granted solely for use by Paul Martin in his
Inspire series and may not be replicated elsewhere.

To all you busy youngsters out there.
May you receive all of the good things
that God has in store for you!

Be inspired!

ACKNOWLEDGEMENTS

I would like to thank my wonderful wife Deb, my bestest friend for putting up with me! You are my Sweetie and I treasure you. We share a precious history of memories made together, of travels, ups and downs and fun times. I love you!! You are the most genuine, gentle and kind person I know. Thank you for believing in me!

Thank you to Alfie for taking a look at these books and giving me some handy tips on making sure it relates to people of your age. Thank you to Henry for having some helpful things to say for improving my sentences. You truly are an awesome author!

Thank you to Mum & Dad for your prayers and support over the years. Your listening ears and wise words have kept me going through the difficulties! Thanks so much for going through all my books and checking them for issues.

Thank you to Simon Genoe for your encouragements and being a brilliant leader whom I am constantly learning from.

Thank you to Carlton Baxter for being a great support to me. You are a great source of strength to me, solid and reliable.

Thank you to Richard Lyttle for the great photo that you took of me! Perfect for the back cover pic!

Thank you to Amy Walters for your light bulb line drawing, which has become a logo for my Inspire books. I love the prophetic insight that comes through your art and design work. You are truly gifted.

...and thank you for buying this devotional! I wrote it so that you will find strength and freedom in Jesus to live your life to the full as you depend on God for so much!

ABOUT THIS BOOK

This book is all about identity. If you've ever wondered, or asked yourself "who am I?" you'll find it's normally a question that leads to a journey. We discover a certain amount of security and worth when we understand the answer to this most basic of questions. Everyone is searching for answers. People who go on from University often consider taking a year out. Gap years are popular in helping students to discover their "calling" in life. Some people have even been known to take a break from work, travelling to far away countries in order to "find themselves;" whilst others look into their ancestry, researching their family tree for answers.

If you were invited on to a quiz show and asked questions about yourself, how do you think you would do? "I ought to be the one who knows my self the best!" we say. So why is it that we don't always feel we do?

There's a well-known text in the Bible written in the Psalms chapter 139. It talks about the truth that God knows us, all about us, our identity, abilities, our ways and even our thoughts. Essentially it gets us to think about the questions we have about life. I believe reading it will help you to discover some fresh insights about who you are.

This book has 40 devotionals and is handy to read each day. There are other bits too. I've called them prayer spaces. These will help you to connect with God. They have bits to write in, to think about and draw as you respond to God in your prayer times; and if you're not familiar with talking to God, hopefully they will be a way to help you start.

I believe God wants to use these devotions to reveal some of the things He wants you to discover about yourself. He loves to talk in ways that suit us. Maybe He will get some words to "jump out" at you as you read and you'll realise their significance. It might be that as you are drawing, a picture comes to mind that communicates a concept that God wants show you. Perhaps as thoughts come to mind something will "click" and you will suddenly understand more. I'm praying for you! I hope that this book helps you to gain greater comfort in knowing who you are in God.

PSALM 139

To the choirmaster. A Psalm of David

¹ You have searched me, LORD and You know me.
² You know when I sit and when I rise;
You perceive my thoughts from afar.
³ You discern my going out and my lying down;
You are familiar with all my ways.
⁴ Before a word is on my tongue,
You LORD, know it completely.

⁵ You hem me in behind and before,
and You lay Your hand upon me.
⁶ Such knowledge is too wonderful for me,
too lofty for me to attain.

⁷ Where can I go from Your Spirit?
Where can I flee from Your presence?
⁸ If I go up to the heavens, You are there;
if I make my bed in the depths, You are there.
⁹ If I rise on the wings of the dawn,
if I settle on the far side of the sea,
¹⁰ even there Your hand will guide me,
Your right hand will hold me fast.

¹¹ If I say "Surely the darkness will hide me
and the light become night around me,"
¹² even the darkness will not be dark to You;
the night will shine like the day,
for darkness is as light to You.

¹³ For You created my inmost being;
You knit me together in my mother's womb.
¹⁴ I praise You because I am fearfully and wonderfully made;
Your works are wonderful,
I know that full well.
¹⁵ My frame was not hidden from You
When I was made in the secret place,
when I was woven together in the depths of the earth.
¹⁶ Your eyes saw my unformed body;
all the days ordained for me were written in Your book
before one of them came to be.

¹⁷ How precious to me are Your thoughts, God!
How vast is the sum of them!
¹⁸ Were I to count them, they would outnumber the grains of sand.
When I awake, I am still with You.

¹⁹ If only You, God, would slay the wicked!
Away from me, you who are bloodthirsty!
²⁰ They speak of You with evil intent;
Your adversaries misuse Your name.
²¹ Do I not hate those who hate you, LORD,
And abhor those who are in rebellion against You?
²² I have nothing but hatred for them;
I count them my enemies.
²³Search me, O God, and know my heart;
Test me and know my anxious thoughts.
²⁴See if there is any offensive way in me,
and lead me in the way everlasting.

GOD'S SEARCHLIGHT

"O Lord, You have searched me and known me!"   (Psalm 139:1)

Imagine you were given the opportunity to choose a superpower; just one ability, anything at all. What would you go for? I know this might take some serious thought, so take your time! For instance, there are the well-known powers such as flying, crawling up walls, super strength, producing ice from your hands, invisibility, mind reading and those sorts of things. Then there are the more unusual ones, like teleporting, power absorption and shape shifting. So many super powers and each one is different!

I know this might sound super boring as he's one of the more underrated superheroes, but I'd like to be like Aquaman! Why? Just because I can't swim! Obviously they are not real, but all of these superheroes have one thing in common: their true identity is kept hidden from most people. I expect if you were to have a superpower, you would keep it a secret too. Why? I guess it would make you more vulnerable to your enemies and the fame would force you to lead a secret life anyway?

I know the superpower thing isn't real, but maybe there are times when we feel that people don't really know who we are. Perhaps you're thinking to yourself "I don't even know who I am either!" It can take time to understand what we are actually like, as there are so many influences around us trying to mould us into a particular shape. Therefore answering the question "Who am I?" can be a difficult one. Identity is more than just having a passport, being born in a certain location or supporting a particular football team. These can communicate something about us, but actually knowing who we are deep inside is altogether more tricky.

Have you ever wondered what God actually thinks about you? We read the words *"O Lord, You have searched me and known me."* Could it be that God actually knows us better than we know ourselves? The word for "searched" takes the idea of examining closely, where God searches our hearts and even knows the reasons why we do things. He goes that deep. So those things that lay hidden inside us, God knows about. You have talents that lay sleeping which are waiting to be discovered. Good character inside you that reflects God's heart of love, mercy and kindness also awaits the opportunity to be revealed; He sees it all.

For the next 40 days we're going on a journey of discovery; both discovering who we are, but also who God is and our relationship with Him. When God searches our hearts it's for a reason: so that He might draw us towards Him. As this happens He will naturally transform us. God works in us to change us, to strengthen our confidence and to stir a loving compassion in our hearts that causes us to become who He made us to be. He knows how to draw the best out of us.

So my question to you is this… will you let God in to search your heart? Think about that for a moment. God who is holy, loving and pure will see what you are like on the inside. He sees it anyway, but He really wants to invite you to see what He finds, so that together you and Him can become close. There will be some things that He wants to help you with, such as hurts that need healing and attitudes that He can shape. Yes it may be a little bit painful at times, yet He will only lead you through these in order to help you, to comfort you and to set you free. So don't hold back, you can trust God to work powerfully in your life and you will be better for it!

Can you commit to pray this with me? *Father God I don't want to hold anything back from You. Thank You that You are a good, loving and pure Father who wants the best for me. Come and do what You want to in my life. Examine my heart and show me what You find. Please shine Your light on the dark places of my heart that I keep hidden. I thank You that Your love for me is not dependant on my heart, but rather on Your loving kindness. Please change what needs changing, show me what I'm good at and lead me to know what You want for my life. In Jesus' name!*

FINDING POTENTIAL

#Day2

"O Lord, You have searched me and known me!"   (Psalm 139:1)

One of the interesting things I remember learning from my school days was in my Physics class on the subject of energy. There are different types of energy that an object will generate depending on what's happening to it. So if you are heating a pan, that object will begin to possess thermal energy. When you pick up that pan, that movement produces kinetic energy. If you had the know-how, you could build a wind turbine to convert the kinetic (movement) energy of the wind into electrical energy. All very interesting, but there is one type of energy that has always intrigued me: potential energy. Say I had a cup of water and I placed it on the middle of a table, it would probably not have much potential energy. Nothing much can happen to it there.

However if I were to place that cup of water on the edge of a table or even on someone's head, suddenly it has a lot more potential! If I were to tell that person a well-timed joke, the kinetic movement of their body as they laughed uncontrollably at my very funny joke would convert that into umm... well I only got a C in Physics, so we'll probably leave it there!

What exactly is God looking for when it says *"You have searched me and known me"*? Doesn't God know everything? So why does He need to search for it? I believe that one of the things He is looking for inside of us is potential. Potential is something that each one of us has which relates to the possibilities ahead of us, who we might be, or what we might achieve. It's there already stored up and it's waiting to be unleashed.

Maybe you're an artist and He sees what beautiful designs you can create, a mathematician and He is going to develop your mind for problem solving. Perhaps He sees a kindness in you that He delights to see you express? Maybe you are a deep thinker that can communicate complex ideas in a way that anyone can understand. Perhaps you are sporty and are born to win! Potential. Things that have not yet taken place, a history that has not yet been written. Does God search our abilities and see if we have the character to handle it? We're all a work in progress! But it's not just your role in life that God is interested in. As I said yesterday, He is interested in us because He wants to draw us toward Him.

God searches us to discover if there is the potential that we will get to know Him better. He is motivated by love. He's already thinking about you. Is there a potential in your heart to move towards Jesus? Imagine a school friend that you didn't know too well asked you out on a date. They'd be asking because they were motivated by love and interested if you like them. A boyfriend or girlfriend relationship is a closer bond than two people who just know each other. They want to spend more time with you, to talk and be together; when you are apart, you're thinking of each other. There's a potential relationship between you and God, where He has already seen you, loved you and wants to be close.

How then do I discover my potential? It's really important to say that our potential finds its best fulfilment when it's a part of God's plan for our lives. This is a journey of discovery that begins with an open heart to God, asking "God what do you want for my life?" He wants to reveal this to you along the way; and at the right time, God will add his kinetic energy bringing to life your potential. Often we don't know what we're made of, which is just as well that God does know. As you spend time with God, He will often hint at the things that you will do in the future and the talents that you have that are currently undiscovered. I've always loved drawing, but it was only when I was forced to pick up a paintbrush for GCSE art that I discovered I was a really good painter! Sometimes God causes circumstances that we don't expect in order that we can find out things about ourselves that we didn't know, but He knew all along!

Over the page is a prayer space to begin to discover the potential that God has stored up for you. Why not take some time to think it over with God?

Things I am best at

Creative things I like to do

What I love to spend my free time doing

Books that I read

My prized possessions

People I admire

Jobs that I think are worthwhile

Things people do that annoy me

Subjects at school I find tough

Bad attitudes I have that I need to deal with

What I would love to be doing in 10 years' time . . .

PRAYER SPACE

Take a look at those things over the page. What things would you like God to develop? Why not choose one thing you are good at, a skill you want to excel in and ask God to increase your potential in that? Then look at the things you feel you are not very good at and ask God to help you understand them more so that they can be improved upon?

FALSELY ACCUSED

#Day3

"O Lord, You have searched me and known me!" (Psalm 139:1)

Have you ever been punished for a crime you didn't commit? Maybe you feel there's a group of people who have the wrong idea about you? Perhaps you've experienced a situation where you just happened to be in the wrong place at the wrong time, with the wrong people? And now you've been associated with a deed you had nothing to do with. You're believed to be guilty even though you didn't do it. Oh the injustice!!

I remember an incident happening to me at school that went like this... I was minding my own business when two of my friends came running round the corner of the school building. I ran up to them and noticing they were out of breath, wondered what was going on. It was then that the headmistress came out of the building and she was raging! Next thing I know we were all getting a telling off by the headmistress, before she dished out our punishment. The following half hour was spent with each of us standing in silence in the assembly hall until lunch time was over! The exact details of what happened are a little sketchy as this happened over thirty five years ago, but I'm sure I was innocent!!

If my headmistress had known me a bit better, she would have discovered that I was actually a really well behaved young lad who avoided any kind of naughtiness at all costs. Sometimes people who don't know us well label us, or associate us with things that are not a true reflection of who we are. It doesn't seem fair and we just wish someone would set the record straight!

There are others who compare us to people or things that we would rather they didn't. I remember being called the name of a character on the TV and I hated it. I was nothing like that person! The trouble is we can sometimes feel others will link us to those we're being compared to and inside we're crying out saying "I'm innocent of these accusations! I'm not what you think I am."

So far we've said about this verse that God really knows us, our secret identity (if you like) and that God sees our potential, the person you and I can be. But there's something else that God wants you to know. He wants to reassure you that He cannot misunderstand you. He's not blindsided by people's efforts to define you, their careless words or ignorance. So if you're feeling misunderstood, just because people don't get you, God has searched you, He knows the truth. Nothing is hidden from Him.

As he writes Psalm 139 it's like the writer is saying "These people are accusing me of things I haven't done! But God you know me! You can even read my mind, so You know for sure what the truth is!" We are going to discover that even if you don't know God yet, you and He have a history. Isn't it amazing that He gets us? We can come to Him and immediately He is up to speed with who we are. How reassuring that there is someone who can set the record straight!

Maybe you're concerned about the false things people have said about you. God doesn't see you that way. You can walk tall, even when people lie about you. You can be secure in the knowledge that God defends those who honour Him with their lives; and He always looks out for His children. People can falsely accuse us, or put us into a box; but they can't take away the truth of who we really are. God sees who you are; both the good and the not so good. Whatever He sees, He invites us to come close to Him. You can be yourself with God, since He knows it anyway. You can talk normally and honestly, aware that you can't shock God!

Let's come to God then and ask Him to show you how He really sees you. *Father God. Thank You that You sent Jesus to bring me close to You. I want to know what You see in me. Help me to see beyond the labels and lies that people use to describe me. You really know me! Please reveal to me what You love about me. In Jesus' name! (Have a look over the page!)*

PRAYER SPACE

Using the lettering shown here why not write out an encouraging Bible verse? Here's a good one:

Isaiah 43:1 "I have called you by name. You are mine."

As you write, think about the words and what they mean as God speaks them to you.

PRAYER SPACE

CLOSE BY

#Day 4

"You know when I sit and when I rise."　　　　　(Psalm 139:2)

Here's a riddle for you:

> Every day I appear, I'll sit at your feet.
> All day I follow, in cold or in heat.
> I'm as big as you are, but I don't weigh a thing.
> Move fast or slow I'll promise to cling.
> What am I?

I'll tell you in a moment! I want you to think of a person that you would love to spend the whole day with. Imagine you had "access all areas" to someone famous that you've always wanted to meet! You can learn a lot about a person if you just followed them around all day. If you stuck to them like glue, you'd discover how busy they were, the places they went to, who their friends were, what interested them on the TV, the things they valued, what they laughed at, as well as what they liked to snack on during the day! If you did this regularly, over time you'd begin to feel a part of that person's life.

Want to know the answer to the riddle? I'm sure you've guessed that it is a shadow! A bit like a shadow God is following our ways, always with us, closer that we think, even closer than your breath and He knows every detail. In our sitting down to rest and our rising to get something done, He knows it.

But why is God so close? What is He so interested in? Some people think wrongly of God that He is there to check up on us, like a strict school teacher, waiting for us to do wrong so He can add it to a list in His book. Let me tell you that is not why He is close by! Motivated by love, God is interested in the details of our lives. He sees the things that cause us pain, the challenges we face and the struggles of our lives and wants us to know that He knows about them too.

Maybe you've been practising a particular dance routine that you are struggling to get right for a performance; what if God were to tell you that He loved seeing you dance today and that you are really gifted at it. How would that make you feel? Maybe you would feel encouraged to not give up but to see this as part of who God has made you to be. Or perhaps you're wondering if you should still go to the youth group as you feel that no one notices you? What if God were to say that you are actually a key part of that group and things really aren't as good when you're not there.

Sometimes we don't always see ourselves in the right light. We put down our abilities and think we're not so good. Of course you might not be the finished product or at the level that you want to be yet, but God is with you in the process saying, "This is part of My plan for your life. Keep it up!" Or there may be times when you feel you don't contribute much when you're out with the group; maybe you've been labelled the quiet one as you are a bit shy. God is there too, and doesn't leave you (just like your shadow doesn't!). He wants you to see that He has noticed great things about you, things that He doesn't want you to give up on.

It is out of love that God takes a close interest in you and me. He really notices and cares about you! Psalm 56:8 says *"You have taken account of my wanderings; put my tears in your bottle"* which describes how tenderly God loves you. He feels the pain that we feel, and sees the times we are moved to tears, in heartbreak, sadness or pain. It registers with God who is so much closer than we think. Maybe this is a good moment to just stop and be aware of how close He is.

Lord Jesus. I thank You that You are my friend and that You are for me. I believe that You are alive and with me here now. Please make me aware of how close You are to me as I spend some time thinking about You...

Have a look over the page to take a bit more time being close to Jesus.

PRAYER SPACE

On the page opposite are different starting points for talking to God.

Have a read of them and see if one or more of them spark some thoughts on a conversation you can have with God. For example, "May my meditation on Your words be pleasing to You," might lead you to think deeply on some of God's words and share with God what comes to mind.

Maybe after what you have just read, you want to offer something heartfelt to God? Perhaps you feel inspired to write a poem, or simply to sing a song you know. This space on both pages is yours just to write or draw as you feel inspired to; thoughts to God or even replies you feel are from Him. Sometimes I just listen to a song and start drawing shapes as I consider God and Him being close to me. Often the results are surprising! Why not give it a try?!

May my meditation on Your words

be pleasing to You

What is it that You are saying to me?

It's Your breath in my lungs

So I'll pour out my praise to You

I'll bring You more than a song

What can I give

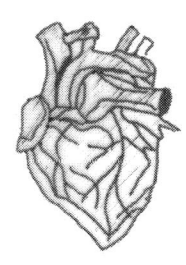

Lord I give You my heart

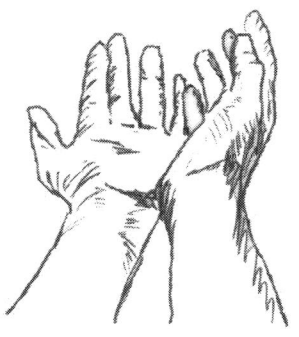

to You my King?

GETTING CONNECTED

#Day5

"You perceive my thoughts from afar."   (Psalm 139:2)

I once was speaking at a high school assembly of about 500 pupils and I really needed to get their attention. So I began my talk by saying, "I am about to read the minds of not just one person, not two, or even three people. I am going to read the minds of everyone in this room!"

Bold claims, I'm sure you will agree! You won't be surprised to hear that there were no gasps of wonder from my audience; more like mumbles of disbelief at my words. Well the first part was fairly easy, as I performed a simple "mind reading trick" on stage (it's not actual mind reading, it just appears that way!) accurately predicting what animals my three volunteers were thinking of. Then returning to my final claim of being able to read the minds of everyone in the room... "Now I can tell what you are thinking," I said, "You are all thinking 'How on earth did he do that??!'" No one could deny it!

Some people think they need to have a special connection for God to know what's on their minds; whilst others see God as being far away and distant from any communication or knowing what they're going through.

How can God be close enough to know what we're thinking; and yet be far away, both at the same time?" Sometimes it's only by using contradictory language that we can begin to understand about God's extraordinary nature. Being close yet far communicates the greatness of God, who can be both in deep space and also at the same time within your heart. The God of the heavens in all His vastness is close enough to get to the very core of who we are.

You might think that such a vast God wouldn't have time to stop and think about you and me, but there is a carefulness about God's actions where it says of God *"You perceive my thoughts from afar."* To perceive is to examine a person's motives (what drives their reasons for their thoughts) the deep things we think that come from the heart. The God of the universe is searching for you. He wants to connect with you on a deep level.

I'm sure you know this, but God can actually hear your unspoken prayers. You can pray to Him using your mind and He hears. So imagine you're in the exam room feeling stressed, He will hear you and help you. Or you're walking down the street and want to talk to God, but don't want to pretend you are using a hands-free device. He will hear your thoughts directed towards Him.

But more than that, because God searches our thoughts, He knows what we need even before we ask Him (Matthew 6:8). I have known so many times when I have wondered about the solution to a problem, only to discover the answer is waiting for me the very next day! Before I even asked for it! I always remember to thank God for those things, acknowledging that we are doing life together and that I can't do it without Him. You see God wants a relationship with you. When you connect with God regularly and often in whatever form that takes, words or no words, thoughts, drawings, dances, or just being aware that He is close, you develop an affinity with Him.

If God is aware of our thoughts, how much easier it is to talk to Him! We can involve Him in our day, and throughout the day make comments to Him; saying we love Him, thanking Him for those random moments that make life easier, sharing our concerns about what's coming up or bringing to mind someone who needs Him.

Father God. I thank you that I have a connection with you; because of Your Son Jesus, you have brought me close! Thank you that You even examine my thoughts and that I can share the moments of my day with you too. May tomorrow be a day that we share together! In Jesus' name!

FINDING PURPOSE

#Day 6

"You discern my going out and my lying down."   (Psalm 139:3)

When you're going through school it can feel a little suffocating having to do the same as everybody else. You have to wear the same uniform, go to the same classes, go through the same procedure of tests or exams and follow the same rules.

Yet as you progress through school, you begin to discover things you are good at. You connect with friendship groups and you develop certain abilities that are unique to you. You might be top of the class in Maths, but lagging behind the rest in Physical Education, or successful in your Chemistry experiments, but what shall we say "Je ne sais pas?" in languages. As a result, you progress through the years choosing subjects that fit who you are. Hopefully at some point there will emerge a purpose to the whole education process. Towards the end, school might even feel a lot less like a sausage factory where everyone comes out the same and more like God's create-your-own gingerbread man workshop.

People go about their busy lives trying to get through the day, unaware of what life has for them, in their "going out." As humans we lie down to recharge the batteries and sleep, then rise to go to school for lessons, to spend time with friends, to go to church, to the shops, the park or wherever. Day after day goes by. Week after week disappears. There are events to look forward to like Christmas, the summer, your birthday, or when something else special is happening. Yet in the dull moments things can appear to be a bit random, where it seems we just decide things at a whim. We can wonder "is it all meaningless?" Will what we are doing actually work towards achieving anything beyond exam results? However, behind the scenes a purpose for our life is unfolding.

God has a purpose in the things that you are doing, even if they seem boring, arduous and uninteresting to you. He is mindful of your ways and is using those things to create a work in you.

God is present in your working, Philippians 2:13 says *"It is God who works in you to will and to act according to His good purpose."* This describes how He leads our desires to do things, so that we might fulfil His purposes! Maybe He has whispered an idea into your mind like, "You're really good at this…" (whatever talent that is) and you have gone on to develop that ability all the time thinking it was all your own plan! It goes on to say in Philippians *"Do everything without complaining or arguing"*! Be aware that even in the tasks that don't interest you, God is using them to draw out value in your life as part of His shaping of you. The best leaders are those who know how to serve; thinking of others first, they put in the effort where others don't. So those things like clearing away after dinner, waiting in line or doing homework aren't worthless to God.

What does the word "discern" mean? It means to analyse, to measure off; not quite like a science experiment though! When I think about buying a gift for my sons, I begin to think about their ways, what they tell me about and things they like to do. I buy something that suits them through what I know. God in the same way analyses our "goings," understanding both our ways and our thoughts in order to guide them.

You have a loving God who is discerning your present to shape your future. To start with you are unique! And God shapes you to bring about something very precious, unlike any other before you. If God were to talk about you to someone else, He'd be saying "Take a look at… (insert your name) look at how wonderful they are. Have you ever seen anyone like them??"

Father God I have to say sorry for the times I have complained and resisted, not understanding that You have been working in my life. Thank You that You know just what I need, both now and for the future. Thank You that You are shaping me into someone very rare. I submit my life to You to do what You want to. In Jesus' name!

JUST THE WAY I AM?

#Day7

"You are familiar with all my ways." (Psalm 139:3)

I used to have a cat who was a creature of habit. It was one of the ways we got to know him and his character. Once he had finished his food (if he didn't sick it up), he would rub his feet beside the bowl like he was digging a hole. If I was making ham sandwiches, he would rub his body past my legs and look up at me making his eyes really big until I gave him some ham and one slice was never enough! He would also use the exact same route to get across the grass every day. If I hadn't mown the lawn for a few weeks there would be a trail of flat grass indicating the daily route he took.

I expect you have your own particular ways too? Maybe you organise your clothes in a certain way in your wardrobe, keep a secret diary, spread jam on your toast in a certain manner or keep to a particular morning routine. We all have our ways! And the older you get, the more likely you are to get set in a certain way of doing things! It's normally our family that really get to experience our weird habits simply because they are closest to us; ways which tend to come about by repetition. These just seem to be the handiest way of doing things, so we do them again regularly.

God is familiar with our ways because He doesn't leave us. He knows us in our daily routine; and much like family He lives with us in the day to day. Family can be the first to notice when something is up with us, even if we don't say a thing; but sometimes those closest to us can miss these clues too, much to our frustration! We want people to notice when we're hurting, annoyed or struggling without us having to say as much!

Maybe your way is to go quiet when you're upset or do the opposite and flare up in anger? Perhaps it's worse and when your emotions are running high and your mind turns to negative options, such as comfort eating, self-harming, addictive behaviours or something else? It's easy to say "That's just who I am. These are my ways," ways which aren't missed by God. There are times when He wants you to hear Him whisper your name to remind you who you really are. He notices those feelings that lead to negative ways; yet He lovingly says to us, "This is not who you are."

Maybe those things aren't an issue for you, but we can all be threatened by the potential to unknowingly take on negative ways; ways that will control us if we let them. As creatures of habit it's easy to pick up ways that were nothing to do with us to start with. We've just learned them, acquired from those around us, or developed in the heat of reacting to events going on in our lives. Now they have become our method of coping.

Although everyone exercises the freedom to do negative things, these ways often produce the opposite of the freedom we are looking for. "It's my life. I can do what I want" we might say. Yet the ways of negative thinking, rages and addictions actually have the effect of controlling us, stealing our freedom. They are poison to us. These ways will control your mood and your thinking, but don't actually bring the relief or joy that you long for. We think we have freedom, but it leads to captivity!

It's easy to think that freedom is the choice to live our own way and do whatever we please; but true freedom exercises the power to reject those poisonous ways that promise to thrill, but actually cost us the inner joy and happiness that we value so much.

Father God. You know who I am. You even know my fingerprint! Thank you that You long for me to discover my true identity, made when You shaped my fingers. Please lead me away from negative pursuits. Thank You Jesus that Your death and resurrection bought me the power to have the freedom to reject addictions and the pull of negative behaviours. Cause me to become aware of who You have made me to be. In Jesus name!

FINISHING OUR SENTENCES

#Day8

"Before a word is on my tongue
      You, Lord, know it completely."   (Psalm 139:4)

Have you ever wondered what your pet dog would say to you if he or she could speak? It would be bizarre, but imagine your goldfish found his voice and jumped out at you and saying "Can you please change the channel on the TV? This documentary on sharks is making me nervous." You'd probably think you needed more sleep, or at least you might think about entering the fish into a talent competition. I used to watch my cat sitting, staring back at me. He always looked like he was plotting something, waiting for me to leave the room or something. I wished he would reply to me in more than just a meow. As humans we are created uniquely different to all the other mammals in a number of ways; one of them is that we can talk and communicate with complex ideas.

We have been created to communicate to God in a deeper way. Our speech is a powerful thing, it is instant; yet communicates thoughts made at lightning speed so that what comes out has meaning to those listening. It tells others some of what's going on inside, depending on how we feel and our inner wants and desires. What we say can be affected by tiredness, stress, whether we trust the person we're talking to or not and will be influenced by the faith and inner conviction that we have.

Complex though it may be, here we discover that there are no secrets with God! He knows it all and He knows what stirs us to say things to Him or to others. He understands the origin of our words and the motivations behind what we say. He is ready with a reply before we have uttered a word! We don't even have to speak for God to know all about it, and our intentions (whether they are good or bad). He knows the background to every situation. He can read us like a book!

All this poses an important question. Why then talk to God when He already knows what we are going to say? If God knows it, do we even have to communicate it? The beauty of this is that yes God can often answer a prayer of ours before we ask it (Matthew 6:8). It's like when a couple who have been together for so long that they know what the other is going to say. They find themselves finishing the other's sentences without even realising they are doing it! This kind of interaction where God is answering our prayers even before we ask it comes when we know God intimately; when our relationship is already built on a foundation of communication. Time has been invested into that relationship because it is something we value.

It's like the couple who give each other valentine's cards when they have been married for 50 years, or the son who always gives his mum a kiss before going off to school. In both cases their love is obvious because of the relationship they have, yet actually making the effort to express that love, somehow cements it further and is a gift given. It's then from this deep bond that we do things we know the other would like even before they ask.

It's easy to forget to talk to God. After all He knows our address and what we are going to say? Right? He knows that we love Him? We're sending Him good thoughts... right? I guess I just want you to answer me this... Of all the things that you do in the day; would you rather God be with you in all of them? Would you rather He is nearby as a close friend giving you help and strength, as opposed to being distant from you because you forgot about Him? At various times it's possible to know Jesus so well that you know what He is going to say to you next.

Maybe there's a commitment you would like to make with Jesus? One where you develop the depth of your conversations with God; where you start to know what He is saying to you? Over the page is a prayer space to help you develop your friendship with Jesus.

PRAYER SPACE

Dear Lord Jesus.

I think it's time that I made a commitment to You that I intend to keep. I want to stay in close communication with You. This is what I promise so that my daily bond with You will grow...

PRAYER SPACE

God loves to reply to us when we talk to Him. Take some time to be quiet and ask God to speak to you. If you have access to music, why not look up the song "Good, good Father," by Chris Tomlin. Then begin writing a letter from Jesus to You. Remember God wants to encourage you!

Dear

With lots of love

Jesus.

ENCLOSED BY GOD

#Day9

"You hem me in behind and before,"   (Psalm 139:5)

Are you the adventurous type? I'm thinking of those outdoorsy activities like rock climbing, abseiling, or jumping out of an aeroplane (with a parachute)? You know, brave pursuits that contain the element of danger? Well there is one such "fun" activity that I am never going to try. Even if you were to offer me a million pounds, you would not be able to make me do the pastime I'm thinking of. It's the activity of potholing. What, you ask, is potholing? I suppose you would call it extreme caving. Where you crawl down into a hole in the ground and you keep crawling as the space you crawl through gets smaller and smaller.

I've seen it on TV and it looks super scary, as people go one behind the other, on their stomachs squeezing through tight rocky crevices with just the torch on their helmet as their source of light. My biggest question about it all is "What if I get stuck? What if my shoulder seizes up or something? Or I get scared and freak out in a confined space? Who then is going to get me out? Would everyone have to reverse out??"

I guess the feeling of being in an enclosed space surrounded by rock makes me uneasy! The idea of being "hemmed in" in this verse can sound like a negative thing, trapped with nowhere to get out. This is not what is meant here, since we're told that being hemmed in by God enables Him to know us in a wonderful way. Is He around us like a bubble? Not really, that's too impersonal for God. It actually means something very friendly and positive; literally "You enclose me." This picture communicates "a surrounding" by God, yet see it in the friendliest of terms. Being bigger than us, He reassuringly wraps around us, making us feel secure in the knowledge that He is close.

Yet there's even more to it than that! It says *"You hem me in behind and before,"* meaning that He's got your back and He goes before you. When someone says "I've got your back," they are telling you that they will remain close looking out for you, thinking of your protection. There are times when negative things come at us that we aren't ready for. God is behind us shielding us when attacked. God also goes before us to check the way ahead. He guides our steps, preparing the way ahead helping us to avoid the pitfalls of life that may lay ahead. He loves to speak to us about what's ahead, encouraging us and preparing us to recognise the way He is working in our lives.

With God we are covered. He sticks with us as the most faithful friend; but remember who God is. He is the awesome and mighty Creator of the universe. If you know Jesus, your identity is as a friend of God! He placed the stars into space and multiplied 5 loaves and two fish to feed 5,000 people. He is the commander of the armies of heaven, and the One who is so utterly holy that no-one can look at Him in His full glory and live. Yet He will come close enough to enclose us, if we invite Him to.

Yesterday we talked about entering into conversation with God in a deeper way. One of the benefits of this is that you become the guy or girl that God wants to hang out with. As a result of our conversations with God, we have the Almighty with us. There is no greater identity than knowing that we are called a friend of God. Get to grips with that. Not only does God love you, He likes you too! He wants to be around you even more than you want Him! This is His choice, not because He has to.

Lord God Almighty. I want You to be with me in everything I do. I thank You that You want to hang around with me! Thank You that I can walk down the street, knowing You're near, behind me and before me. I know that when I have You with me I can be an enormous blessing to others. May I be more sensitive to the times when You want me to know that You are real close, that I may know what You are up to. In Jesus' name!

THE TOUCH OF GOD

#Day10

"You hem me in behind and before,

and You lay Your hand upon me"   (Psalm 139:5)

I don't know if you've ever noticed, but the power of a hug can never be underestimated. It can do wonders for your day! I read somewhere that regular hugs keep people together. Apparently 8 seconds is the kind of time you need to spend per hug if you want to maximize the benefits of a hug. People like a good hug. It makes us feel wanted and loved; and builds a deeper connection with that person you are hugging.

Hugs normally surface in times of emotional vulnerability such as being eliminated from the X Factor, after you've fallen off your bike, received your exam results or won the lottery. Of course there are other times when hugging is just a natural expression of friendship. Unfortunately there are also times when hugging isn't appropriate, such as during a professional game of chess, where the other person has decided on a handshake or when a person is about to sneeze.

A hug is more than just about physical touch. As has been said, you wouldn't just hug anyone, unless you were giving out free hugs. Touch is necessary in our physical world. It shows that you care to a particular person and brings a connection with someone that goes beyond words. Physical contact helps a person to feel loved, more than just being told as much. We read the words, *"You lay Your hand on me,"* which highlights a physical aspect of God's pursuit of us, where we can actually feel that He is close. God can become so close that you can actually feel that He is in the room!

In the Old Testament when it uses the phrase *"the hand of the Lord was upon..."* it communicates how a person was being helped to success by God in a supernatural way. It signifies God's very real blessing on a person helping that person to know He is with them in a very real way.

I remember some years ago making a commitment to God that I would set aside an hour of every day to meet with Him. I would go to my bedroom after dinner, close the door, and sitting on my bed, pick up my Bible and ask the Holy Spirit to be with me. Jesus tells us in John 14:26 that the Holy Spirit will *"teach you all things"* and remind us of everything Jesus taught. So I would open my Bible at the Psalms, Gospels or other places and ask the Lord to teach me and help me to understand more of what I'm reading. I had a journal to write down anything I was inspired by.

But something happened that I wasn't expecting. As I began to think deeply on what I read and talked to God about it, I was often overwhelmed by a strong feeling of love. It was incredible and made my times with God super exciting. Other times a fragrance would fill the room and I would feel that God was really close; inside my chest I felt full of peace and God's power. How could I tell? It was very obvious. I didn't want to leave and one hour seemed to pass like 10 minutes! But it was a felt thing. Like if you turn on a hot water tap; you can feel when it first comes out cold and the temperature change even though the water doesn't look any different. A video camera might not show any difference, but when you are in a room where God is evidently making Himself known, you really feel the difference!

Much like a hug, God wants us to know Him more than just words on a page. He is very real, and when you encounter Him like this you are never the same again! God transforms us with His touch! I am no one special! God gives His Spirit to all who know Jesus (John 7:37-39 and Luke 11:9-13).

Father God. I long to know You close to me, to feel Your love and power in my heart. Thank You that Jesus died for me that I can have peace with You. I ask for the Holy Spirit. Please fill me with Your love and power. Help me to know You are close to me. In Jesus' name!

```
01000111011011110110010000010
00000111011101100001011011110
01110100011100110010000000111
10010110111101110101001001000 00
01110100011011110010000000111
00110110010101100101011010 11
00100000011000010110011001 11
01000110010101110010001000 00
```
DATA COLLECTION `01001000011010010110 1101`

#Day11

"Such knowledge is too wonderful for me," (Psalm 139:6)

The internet is quite incredible. I can't remember how our lives managed to function without it! If you're hungry and can't cook, it's okay. At the press of a button someone will turn up at your door with some cooked pizza. When someone's birthday is coming up, before you buy you can call up reviews and even watch that item being opened and tried out!

A while back I was doing some research online for a car racing set when I logged on to my social media. To my surprise an advert popped up on my social media page with pictures of this same product and a link of where to buy it. At first, I was like "O wow, what a coincidence! Social media is like magic, it knows me so well!" It didn't take me too long to realise that this was no coincidence. "Cookies" were responsible! Not those tasty sweet biscuits with chocolate chips inside, but rather web browsing data that sites use to glean information from us when we're looking to buy stuff. It helps companies tailor their ads to get us to buy from them.

Over the last few days we've been reading this, *"Before a word is on my tongue You, Lord, know it completely. You hem me in behind and before, and You lay Your hand upon me. Such knowledge is too wonderful for me."* The writer is saying "God how could You know me that well?? You know everyone this well! It's enough to blow my mind!" God's knowledge of us far surpasses the information that any internet browser could process.

Stop and think about that for a moment. Is it reassuring to know that God is thinking about you? He has all the up-to-date information on how you're doing. During those times when you're going through a rough situation; it's so comforting when a friend is aware of your distress and shows concern for you. You feel reassured that they will do all they can to help you out. Maybe you have a parent who takes the time to listen as you tell them about some difficulty you are facing; they don't just forget about your troubles, they carry your burdens with them. In the same way like those cookies, God uses the knowledge that He discovers about you to carry your burdens as the very best parent and works on your behalf to turn them for good.

Some people are worried that if God knows all about them, He will also discover the not so good things about them. They are concerned that God will judge them for all the mistakes they have made. The Bible tells us that God reaches out to us *"while we were still sinners"* (Romans 5:8). His first action is to offer us love and to clean up our mistakes. It's only if we reject Him that we come under judgement; yet even then He is still calling us to Him in love. If we are followers of Jesus, there is no longer any judgment against us (Romans 8:1), no penalty due because Jesus has paid our debt.

The writer of this Psalm wants God to search his heart to look for anything that he has done wrong. He believes he is innocent before God, but genuinely wants God to search his heart for any bad motives, thoughts, or plots that are forming inside. The writer would rather be shown them, so that he can be clear of them and be innocent before God, so he welcomes God's data gathering processes.

God wants to take on your burdens, whether troubles you are facing or inner failings that you need forgiven. We can't hide them from God and it is better to let God show you how best to deal with them.

Father God. I'm so glad that You have all the data on me. I am secure in the knowledge that You want what's good for me and not harm. Thank You that You use this information working for my good, according to Your purposes which will fit me like a glove. Rather than fight, I'll surrender to Your ways. Come and work in my heart. In Jesus' name!

PRAYER SPACE

God wants to encourage you, so that you can have insight into what Jesus sees in you. Take time to talk to God and ask Him what good things He sees in you. Then take a look at the words below, deciding how well they describe you by writing a number from 1 to 8 beside each one. If you write a 1 it means the word doesn't describe you that much and 8 that it describes you very well. Obviously a 4 is somewhere in between. Also if a word does not describe you at all, you don't need to put a number next to it. So grade each word and I'll tell you what's next...

Encourager __   Insightful __
Approachable __   Imaginative __
Kind-hearted __   Positive __
Loyal __   Compassionate __
Forgiving __   Christ-like __
Creative __   Honest__
Bright __   Adventurous __
Genuine __   Inspired __
Servant-hearted __   Listener __
Worshipper __   Leader __
Faithful __   Lively __
Giving __   Speaker __
Thoughtful __   Companion __
Bold __   Inventive __
Brave __   Hopeful __
Sensitive __   Skilled __
Thinker __   Expressive __
Practical __   Reliable __
Musical __   Tender-hearted __
Dancer __   Gentle ___
Overcomer __   Caring __
Sporty __   Organised __
Arty __   Trustworthy __
Competitive __   Careful __
Inclusive __   Risk-taker __

PRAYER SPACE

For the next bit you'll need to call up **www.wordart.com** and as you can see it's a word cloud generator. On the left you can see a table that says "Filter, size, colour, angle, font." Type in your words under filter, one per line and put the number you scored for each word in the "size" box next to it.

Put all of the words in and any other *positive* words that come to mind that you feel relate to you (but no negative words!). Also go to options and for the "Words options" have "Repeat" set to "None." Finally press the red "Visualise" button. Does this word cloud describe you well? If it's good, feel free to copy it out in the space below as a reminder of who you are.

REVEALED BY GOD

#Day12

"Such knowledge is too wonderful for me,
too lofty for me to attain."   (Psalm 139:6)

What's your favourite movie? There's a classic film that has got to be in my top 3 best ever movies. I remember staying up late to watch it on the TV one Christmas; and as a lad it set my imagination running wild! The film starred Harrison Ford and was called "Raiders of the lost Ark." It was based on a historical artefact called the Ark of the Covenant (not Noah's Ark), a sacred gold box that contained the 10 commandments. Although the artefact has been historically documented, the film was just a bit of fictional fun, yet was inspired by the real search for this item.

To find the Ark of the Covenant would be incredible, probably the most important archaeological discovery known to man, yet it remains missing to this day. Only God knows its exact location and those whom He chooses to reveal it! Why is this item so precious and sacred? Take a look at Joshua 3:14-17 for an example of the sort of things that happened around those carrying the Ark of God.

Some things in this life are hidden from us, unknowable until they are revealed to us by God. Proverbs 25:2 says, *"It is the glory of God to conceal a matter, to search out a matter is the glory of kings."* I doubt anyone will find the Ark of the Covenant, but there are some things that God actually hides for us to find. Such things may not be easy to come by, or accessible to all, but only those who choose to search them out, honouring them as valuable. What each person values will vary, but when we tap into understanding God's heart, we can discover a whole other realm of precious stuff hidden in God's kingdom.

Maybe you would love to have insight into the goings on in the heavenly realms; to see those things that influence people around you? Perhaps you really want to hear God speak to you or through you to bless other people? Could it be that you need God to deal with some deep things inside, where you have been hurt, yet those emotional wounds appear to be holding you back? Or is it that you just really want to experience God at work in your life in His reality and power?

We read the words, *"Such knowledge is too wonderful for me, too lofty for me to attain,"* where there are things beyond our reach by our own efforts. However, God may choose to reveal them to those who search them out by seeking Him.

To go back to the Ark of the Covenant, in Old Testament times it was situated in the Tabernacle, the meeting place where Moses would see God face to face. Moses would come out of His meetings with God and his face would shine so bright that people couldn't look at him. They got him to put a veil over his face! There is a transformation that takes place when we seek God and find him. You will find yourself being more loving, more confident, more joyful and more connected to God.

It's up to God what He chooses to reveal to you, as His revelation doesn't come through trying hard or having earned a certain level of spirituality. You and I cannot attain it. Yet if we make knowing God better as our goal, He will certainly give us the desires of our heart.

Father God. My desire is to find my identity deeply in knowing You. Thank You that there is a place for me here. Would You awaken my soul to the things of Your kingdom? I want to find my place in all that You have planned for me. I know there is a lot that You want to show me, that I cannot attain by my own research or effort. I value You and the things of Your kingdom and commit to place these above all my other desires. I want to know You more and be known as one who walks with God.
In Jesus' name!

NOWHERE TO HIDE

#Day13

"Where can I go from your Spirit?"   (Psalm 139:7)

I wonder what it would be like to be a fugitive (someone on the run from the government). Let's assume you are a spy in a foreign country! You are desperate to find somewhere to lay low, at least until the search dies down a bit. In this day and age would it be possible to escape detection?

Just think, you can't cross the border to another country as the border controls will check you thoroughly! Using a "borrowed" car would be risky as it would be reported missing. A number plate search would enable the authorities to track your movements all the way to your location. With CCTV in towns watched by staff 24/7 you'll need a disguise. You'd also need to have plenty of cash as using your debit card would flag up your identity and location on banking computer systems. Even having your cell phone on could make your whereabouts obtainable by those with the right technology.

Perhaps you would make it to a remote location, only to arouse suspicion from the locals. Is there anywhere in this modern world to hide?? The writer of this Psalm asks, *"Where can I go from your Spirit?"* Stating that hiding from God too is futile. When it comes to God I can't run, I might as well surrender!!

We can't physically hide from God and as we've seen before, neither can we hide our inner thoughts from Him. He wants us to come genuinely, holding nothing back from Him; surrendering rather than resisting, especially when He wants to highlight something in our lives. I'm sure you've done that thing when you don't want to hear the football results on the TV or purposefully want to ignore someone, where you put your hands over your ears and say, "La la la la" lots of times.

We can get a bit like this with God too, where the Holy Spirit has chosen to point something out about our character or ways which He wants to work on and change; yet our response is to resist and say, "I'm happy the way I am, don't make me uncomfortable." So we avoid God, or even turn away from Him, hoping He will leave us alone. Yet God loves us too much to do that, so He pursues us.

What sort of things am I talking about? It could be a bad attitude that we hold, or a lie that we are choosing to believe which is contrary to God's words. To unfairly judge someone else or tell ourselves that our lifestyle is acceptable to God when the Holy Spirit is whispering otherwise, will lead us in one of two directions. To either rebel against God, or to continue trying to maintain a faith, but lacking in that spiritual passion that makes God come alive inside.

Put simply it's running away or pretending nothing is wrong. In both cases it is living in a fantasy world, believing that God will allow us to come to Him on our terms, when actually deep down we know that something needs to be put right. God doesn't leave us alone and calls us to restore a right relationship with Him. There's no hiding from Him; He knows our address, wherever that might be.

The Holy Spirit is just that, holy; which means He is utterly pure, good and full of truth. He will convict our hearts, raising our conscience to detect an issue. Some people respond to this by trying to dull their conscience to stop it from working so that they can continue doing things that are not pure or good and represent lies that the enemy has fed them.

Father God. I recognise this battle within in my heart, between truth and lies, things holy and those that make me feel unclean. I know it's time to surrender to You, as I know You won't let up on me. I submit to what You have been telling me through my conscience and ask You give me the strength and opportunity to make them right. In Jesus' name! *(PTO)*

Judgmental attitudes

Cast me not away
from your presence,
and take not
Your Holy Spirit
from me.
Psalm 51:10-11

Bad habits

S*!#

Wrong
relationships

PURSUED BY A HOLY GOD

#Day14

"Where can I flee from Your presence?" (Psalm 139:7)

Did you ever play "Kiss chase" in the playground when you were younger? If you're not familiar with this game, it's something I remember in primary school, where normally the boys would run away and the girls would chase. The boys tried their best not to get caught because if they were captured, they would get a kiss from the girl who caught them. Ewwww!! Remember when kisses were like that!?

Much of the time the boys were faster than the girls and so managed to get away. However some of the girls were persistent and resourceful which left unsuspecting boys vulnerable to a surprise kiss!

Generally people who flee, don't want to be caught because they fear the negative consequences. It's possible to be on bad terms with God and to feel this way about Him, fearing that He is chasing us with a big stick! Yet when we are pursued by God it's a lot more like the kiss chase! When God pursues us His children, it's out of a love for us and not in order to strike us down.

We read the words *"Where can I flee from Your presence?"* Why then would the writer want to flee from God? After all God is so loving and kind, He is for us and not against us. When God makes plain to a person how real He is, the Holy Spirit may make them aware of how utterly pure God is too; there's a sudden realisation of standing on holy ground. This can be totally overwhelming, where the ugliness of our own wrongdoing contrasts with the beauty of God in all His holiness.

46

In these rare times where God allows a person to experience His holiness, they catch a glimpse of how far they fall short of being like Him. The heart registers an unworthiness to be close to God and all they can do is wail in despair! The only human response is to run in the other direction! The writer registers this feeling of wanting to flee from God because his natural reaction to God's holy presence is, "This is too much for me to take!! My body can't cope with being this close to a holy God."

Naturally being close to God makes us realise those areas in our lives that need to be cleaned up. Being in someone's company has a powerful effect on how we act. During the time we spend with Him, God will change and transform us into His likeness, which is our true identity; since we are made in the image of God.

As children of God we find ourselves in the process of being made more like Him. Regular times of being close to God will give you an inner longing to be pure, driving you to stay away from those things that tempt toward impurity. It's like you want to preserve a clean heart, because of a longing for God's powerful presence. This is the sacrifice some make, so as not to be the very thing that gets in the way of being in His presence; after all *"the pure in heart shall see God"* (Matthew 5:8).

Perhaps the thought has come to mind "I can never be clean enough to see God!" God knew we'd have this problem as humans. Therefore He sent Jesus to pay for my wrongs and your wrongs, to make us clean so we can approach God at any time. He also sends the Holy Spirit so you can encounter His presence where He will speak and work in your life.

Maybe you never got caught playing kiss chase, but God is intent on catching you more than you know!

Father God, thank You for sending Jesus so that I can approach Your holy presence. Thank You for sending the Holy Spirit that I may encounter You. I choose to put away those wrong things that will hinder our relationship. I choose to invest my time in discovering more of You. Please lead me into Your holy presence, that I may know You more. In Jesus' name.

GOD OF HEAVEN

#Day15

"If I go up to the heavens, You are there;"   (Psalm 139:8)

I've been wondering... You know when a game like football is on. Why do some footballers point to the sky each time they score a goal for their team? Could the answer to this be that they are saying thank you to God for all His blessings in their life? Or perhaps it's an indication that they had divine help in securing victory for their team? Maybe I'll try that next time I do a great assembly or make a good cup of tea.

Yet why point to the sky? Is that where God is? Is He just somewhere in that blue bit? Because I have been up there in an aeroplane and it didn't look too likely. Obviously God is unseen. Then what about beyond the sky, space, stars and planets and stuff?

When some people talk about the heavens, they tend to be referring to one of two places. They'll either be talking about the place where God is (heaven itself) or just meaning "the sky." In Hebrew thinking the physical realm consisted of three places, the sky, earth and water. At the same time they understood there to be this other dimension, a fourth dimension if you like where God exists beyond the restrictions of time, a heavenly realm. Yet why if you were trying to escape God would you go to heaven? It's not like He leaves the place unattended.

God is present and active in both dimensions at the same time. Unfortunately we can sometimes forget this. Have you ever been praying and felt like your prayers were getting nowhere? I remember someone saying how they felt their prayers were just "hitting the ceiling," as if their words had to go somewhere up to get to God. But is God only "up there"?? Of course not!!

We've been reading about how God knows our thoughts and the words we are about to speak before we say them; that He encloses us! Don't be misled to thinking that God is far away! The writer of the Psalms is saying, "God you are as far away as can be, in the furthest realm possible I can think of. If I were to go there You would be there; yet at the same time, right now you are as close to me as my breath."

Does that make you wonder at God's greatness? So vast He's waiting in the distant sunset, so close you'll hear His whisper in your ear. He surrounds us with His wonderful presence by day and night. He moves beyond distance, is not restricted by any physical barriers and is never late when we need to meet with Him. He's always there when we pray. At the right time He allows us to sense He's there. To which we respond "God is in this room!" But really He's always there, we just happened to notice! He's most obvious when in heaven, where His glory isn't as shielded; He can't be missed in His brightness and Majesty. The peace and power of being in the presence of the King of Glory is a wonderful thing.

God is so otherworldly in scope. No size is too big for Him to navigate around or too small for Him to notice. It can only be love that would bring One so mighty to stop for the likes of you and me. He has already demonstrated what He is prepared to do to show us His love and desire for us through His death on a cross.

Why not take a moment to become aware of His presence? The God of heaven wants to make you know He is close; for you to experience a taste of what He's like in heaven.

Holy Spirit of the Living God. I ask you to come close to me and show me more of what Jesus and the Father are like. As I wait for You, please make me aware that You are in the room. Fill this room and fill my heart, let me know of Your desire for me and what You think of me. In Jesus' name!

GRAVE SITUATION

#Day16

"if I make my bed in the depths, You are there."   (Psalm 139:8)

Ever been to a gig? What it would be like to get a VIP pass giving you access all areas, especially if it's your favourite band? What an experience to go backstage and meet your heroes after seeing them play live. Perhaps you'd get to sit and eat in the same room as them as they chill out. Be a part of the banter and hear about how the gig went for them. Maybe there would be a moment to say "hi" and even get an autograph.

Not everyone gets access to such an opportunity, yet your pass identifies you as one to be welcomed by the crew for special treatment. Security won't just let anyone through to take selfies with band members; but they'll pick you out of a crowd of people trying to get backstage because your pass indicates you've been checked beforehand.

What has this got to do with being in the depths?? Well there's a place we will all go to one day which the Psalmist refers to in this verse. It's a place where we need to be identified with God before we get there. The depths can also be translated as a place called "Sheol" or "the grave." In Hebrew times it was understood as a waiting place for the dead, where those who died who knew God would be rescued to be taken up to Him.

The Bible explains two things that happen to those who die that belong to Jesus; two things that appear to be contradictory, but aren't. Whilst dying on the cross, one of the criminals with Jesus says, *"Jesus, remember me when You come into Your kingdom!"* Jesus' reply was, *"Truly I tell you, today you will be with me in paradise"* (Luke 23:40-43). So those who are committed to Jesus immediately go to be with Him in heaven.

Yet the Bible also tells us that when Jesus returns He will give a shout and all the dead believers in Christ will be raised up. So the question is, do we go to heaven or stay in the grave 'til Jesus returns?

The answer is both! On death our spirit, that inner part of us will go to be with Jesus where we will meet Him and enjoy seeing, breathing and touching the spiritual realm of paradise. A perfect place where there is no crying, pain or evil. Meanwhile our physical body remains in the grave, waiting for Jesus' return. Then when Jesus returns our physical body will be raised to life and made perfect, so it won't be like a zombie apocalypse! Our bodies (including those whose remains are no more) will be raised to life, healed and restored to join with the other part of us that has been with Jesus in paradise (1 Thessalonians 4:13-18).

So going back to our access all areas pass at the gig, it's your identity in Jesus Christ that brings you to life again. When your body dies, God remembers those who know Jesus. He will find you and bring you to be with Him, *"if I make my bed in the depths, You are there."* When you are His, there is nowhere where God can't find you.

Having an identity in Christ is not simply accepting a set of beliefs to gain an access pass into heaven. It's a relationship with God, a lifestyle of following Jesus and a worship of Him as the King of Kings. Importantly we learn from the criminal at the cross of Jesus; that this man recognised his deeds deserved punishment and was truly sorry. He also saw Jesus for who He was, innocent and the King of heaven, God Himself. At this last moment his genuine response to Jesus was enough for Jesus to save him.

So the important question for you is this... Is your identity in Christ? Are you a Christian? Have you admitted you have done wrong? Let's face it, we all have, lots of times. Jesus didn't come to rub it in, He came to rub it out! Do you believe Jesus died and rose from the dead? The evidence is there in the Bible to see! And importantly are you prepared to commit your life to discovering more of Jesus and having a friendship with God? Over the page is a prayer space that will take you through beginning your life with Jesus.

PRAYER SPACE

The Bible tells us that God so loved the world (that is us), that He gave His only Son that whoever believes in Him shall not perish but have everlasting life (John 3:16).

Q - Do you believe that God came to earth for you?
Q - Do you believe that Jesus lived and died for you?
Q - Do you believe that God loves you?

The Bible says that no one is perfect; that we have all done wrong and fallen short of God's standard. Heaven is a perfect place where God is, but we being imperfect are separated from God without Jesus.

Q - Do you admit that you have done wrong?
Q - Are you sorry for those things you have done?
Q - Would you like God to forgive you?

The Bible contains eye witness accounts of how the Romans executed Jesus through the torture of nailing Him to a cross (John 19). God purposed this to happen so that ours wrongs could be erased. He rose from the dead three days later demonstrating that He was God's Son (see John 20).

Q – Do you believe Jesus was God's only Son?
Q – Do you believe that He died for you?
Q – Do you believe He rose from the dead?

Jesus said "Whoever wants to become my disciple must deny themselves and take up their cross and follow me." (Matthew 16:24).

Q – Will you receive God's free gift of wrongs forgiven and eternal life with Him in heaven?
Q – Do you choose to live your life for Jesus?

PRAYER SPACE

Whether you've been to church loads of times or never set foot inside a church, God wants you to know Him. When you pray this prayer something will happen. God will come close to you whether you sense Him close or not. He wants you to know that you are His forever!

If you have chosen to follow Jesus, please pray this prayer...

> *Dear Lord God; Almighty God, I come to You as a stranger, but I want to be Your friend.*
>
> *I know that in Your deep love for me You welcome me. Thank You for sending Jesus into the world to show me what You are like. I believe He is Your Son and that He lived on this earth and that He was executed by the Romans. Thank You that You planned this in order that I could be made free; free from the power of the enemy over my life and free to be forgiven for all of my wrongs.*
>
> *I believe Jesus rose from the dead and that I can know Him with me every day.*
>
> *Please forgive me for all the wrong things that I have done. I am truly sorry. In respect for You, I turn away from the wrong things I have done and choose to follow You. Help me to live my life for You.*
>
> *Now I ask You to come and take over my heart and my life. In Jesus' name!*

Once you have taken this step with God, the Bible calls you a child of God *"Yet to all who did receive Him, to those who believed in His name, He gave the right to become children of God"* (John 1:12). This means that you have peace with God; and God as the best loving Father includes you in His family and will guide you in life, protect you and provide for the things you need. This is the start of a wonderful friendship with God!

READY FOR ANYTHING

#Day17

"If I rise on the wings of the dawn," (Psalm 139:9)

Have you ever been up early enough to see the sunrise in the morning? You actually don't have to be up that early to see it and it's quite something to witness as it unfolds. When I was younger we used to get up at around 5am to go away for our summer holidays and avoid the London traffic. As I watched out the window London seemed to be sleeping, very few people around. Then when the sun rose, the street lights that lit the darkness began to fade as beams of light rose from the horizon. It didn't take long for day to begin. The speed of light must be incredible. As dawn breaks, the light that appears can be seen instantly from miles away.

We've been thinking about how there is no place too far to get away from God, *"Where can I go from Your Spirit? Where can I flee from Your presence? If I go up to the heavens, You are there; if I make my bed in the depths, You are there."* There is also no time that God isn't ready for; *"If I rise on the wings of the dawn."*

What does that mean? Birds have wings, but the dawn doesn't! Some concepts are best described using abstract picture language. The writer is bringing to mind the picture of swiftness, like a bird in flight and pairing it with the breaking of dawn. When sunrise appears it covers the land with light at a great speed. It's like something someone would say in the book *The Hobbit*. I can imagine the company of Dwarves, Elves and Hobbits on a journey of escape after a night under the stars, "We must rise on the wings of the dawn!" as they get up at daybreak to continue their flight from their pursuers. It has with it this idea of being early and moving with haste, to have a head start over those they are running from.

Yet if we were to take flight from God, the writer admits that God is always ready. You won't find Him sleeping or having a lay-in. He is with you even at midnight! He's there when you sleep and the first to greet you in the morning, ready to be a part of your day.

God is there to strengthen you in the challenges, to comfort you in the disappointments and to give you hope and a bright future. He is as aware of those around us as He is of you. Involving God in the challenges of your day enables you to have courage as the day unfolds. God is ready as you team up with Him to help with the things that you can't do (James 1:17). When things come at you with great speed they won't take God by surprise. The more you invite God into your day, the more you will notice His invisible hand providing those things that you need at just the right time. God is ready for anything covering your day at the speed of light.

Think about that for a moment... God knows just who you are, your secret identity, He is used to your routine, He sees your ways. God understands your thoughts, knows what you need and what you are about to say. He is working on your behalf at the speed of light to fulfil His purposes. To have one so committed to us, full of justice and love is extremely reassuring. Be comforted by the fact that as you face the unknown of today that you don't face any of it alone.

God is not slow to answer and wants us to live dependent on Him. So how can we involve God in our day? I believe it's more than just a quick prayer in the morning (although that is an excellent start). If we don't have another thought towards Him until the evening, that's a big chunk of relationship that we have missed out on. Talk to Jesus often and regularly, as you communicate with thoughts, words and pictures. When something good comes your way, enjoy the fact that God went ahead and placed it there especially for you. Let your day be filled with a close bond with Him.

Lord Jesus. I thank You that You are alive and with me every day. Father God I love that you provide for the things that I can't do and go ahead of me, leaving good things for me to find. Holy Spirit, You never leave me. I long for more of Your presence in my life. Please make me sense when You are up to something and help me to see You in all of my day. I look forward to noticing when You want my attention. I love you Lord.

FINDING YOUR FEET

#Day18

"if I settle on the far side of the sea,"   (Psalm 139:9)

What's it like to move to a new town or city? To leave the place you've known all your life? The experience of moving away can be an exciting, yet unsettling event, where everything can seem new. You have a new bedroom, a new school, new people to meet, and you feel like you are the newbie. There's so much to learn all at once, the route to school, getting up to speed with subjects and everyone's names, which leads to discovering friends. Once you're in the middle of all of this going on around you, it can leave you asking the question "Where do I find my place in all of this?" You might say "I had an identity back where I was, but now I just don't know who I am or how I fit in."

Perhaps you were a part of a sports team back home, were really involved at church or were a key part of a circle of friends. Maybe as a result of things going on, it has knocked how you feel about yourself. It's possible to feel self-confident because of the things we do rather than who we are. Having a particular role that everyone knows us for can become our identity. When these things are lost, it can seem like a part of us is lost too. If you feel you are lacking a confidence that you once had, God whispers in your ear "I think the world of you! Don't even think about re-inventing yourself to fit in! You are a gifted and beautiful individual full of character. Trust Me to make you shine. I am doing a marvellous work in you."

There's a security in knowing that first and foremost we have a place in God's heart and an identity in His kingdom. Having a relationship with Jesus builds strong blocks of character that strengthen who you are. You can walk boldly and confidently into a room full of people you don't know, because His presence is with you. Finding your feet becomes less uncertain ground, because you first know who you are. You can be brave because you know you don't have to impress anyone, as God is looking out for you.

Today we read the words *"if I settle on the far side of the sea,"* which refers to a place far away, to a new home. The idea goes on to communicate it being a place where God's enclosing presence doesn't leave us alone. Often in times of struggle we have to lean into God more than ever for help and support. In response He can make Himself more real to us, turning what is a challenging time into a very precious one. This can be an opportunity in which you are shaped as a person, where God will actually define you, rather than one where your identity is lost. You'll discover how you function in what God has made you to be, as God brings out the best in you. It's only when we look back years later that we understand how God was working out His ways for our good.

The same God who was with you in your yesterday is with you right now in your today and waiting in your tomorrow. It may be that you will need to be patient as your current set of circumstances unfolds, yet in the meantime you can still know Father God providing for you in all sorts of ways. He wants to calm your fears about tomorrow and to give you the things you need for today.

Father God. I thank You that You have adventures in store for me that I know nothing about. Maybe they are even located on the far side of the sea. I know I can trust that You know best and are working for my good. So I won't shrink back or fear tomorrow. Instead I'll say "Bring it on!" because any adventure with you is better than staying at home and missing out on what you have called me to be.

Lead me in Your way and give me a confidence in You that is secure. In Jesus' name!

HEAVEN'S PLAN FOR YOU

#Day19

"If I rise on the wings of the dawn, if I settle on the far side of the sea, even there Your hand will guide me," (Psalm 139:10)

I remember the first time I really felt homesick. I was on mission in Estonia and we had only been there two weeks! Yet two weeks was enough to do it for me. We had travelled to various places, bedding down on church floors and making use of very basic facilities. In one place where we stayed the water was brown; and before using the toilet for any length of time, you had to check it had a seat, a lock and some paper. To get all three was a luxury!

I could cope with all of the basics alright, but the one thing that made me feel a longing for home was being so far away from those I loved. The distance was crushing. I remember two members of my team, an English girl and a German girl could see that I was a wee bit down and they decided to get everyone to sing happy birthday to me. As the song finished they came up beside me and simultaneously kissed me on either cheek! As I gasped in surprise they immediately shoved a Custard Cream biscuit into my open mouth! A taste of home that was very much appreciated!

Distance from home can do something to us, where we often need more support. Eventually we all have to "fly the nest," like a young bird ready to start out on its own; but until that time, being away from home (although an adventure) can be hard. We read the words of reassurance *"even there Your hand will guide me"* that God is actively influencing and directing us according to His plan. We've already said that the term for God's hand being with us indicates His blessing and help to success. His hand also reassures us that He is close. Like when you were younger and you were out shopping. Holding a parent's hand is comforting for a child. It keeps them close and ensures they don't get lost. There's a powerful song that I believe bits of it communicate the heart of God as a loving Father for His children in times like these. Here's a snippet from it:

Up on the hill across the blue lake
That's where I had my first heart break
I still remember how it all changed
My father said:
"Don't you worry, don't you worry child
See heaven's got a plan for you." [a]

God as a loving Father has His hand upon your life for good. When you feel far away from those you rely upon, God is there holding on to you, not letting go and guiding your steps for good. He will provide comfort for you in those challenging times.

A question a lot of people ask is "How do I know that God is guiding me?" We want reassurance that the choices we make are the right ones for us in those big decisions such as subject options, career choices and relationship dilemmas. When we're facing decisions where the outcome is unknown, we need the certainty of God's help to obey His ways and to enjoy the success that only comes from Him. Much like the song says; it all begins with trusting that God is already working on your behalf.

There will be times in your life where you might find that some decisions are made for you by God; where circumstances have taken you in a certain direction. God wants to release you from the pressure to think it's all up to you to make your future happen. We don't need the blueprint for the next 20 years, just the next step in the decisions we need for today. Take a look at Matthew 6:25-34 where Jesus reassures us that our Heavenly Father is looking out for us in this way.

Over the page is a prayer space to bring to God any big decisions of your life and help you to discover what the next step might be.

PRAYER SPACE

Write in this box any decisions you are facing.

Read Proverbs 3:5-6

Now write out the verse here and as you write it think carefully about each word.

PRAYER SPACE

In what ways do I need to submit to God in this decision? (To submit means to discover, accept and follow God's ways rather than our own).

On a scale of 1 to 10 (one being low and 10 being high) how much do I currently trust God to help me with this decision?

In what ways can I show that I trust God with this decision?

Father God. I am ready to trust You with this decision in my life. I know that You care about what happens even more than I do. I know that You want what's best for me. I don't need to know the outcome yet, just the next step that you want me to take. I thank You that You are a good good Father and that I am loved by You. In Jesus' name.

As you close your eyes, I want you to imagine you are out walking somewhere safe and calm and that at some point Jesus comes walking beside you. As you picture the scene, ask God to speak to you. What is going on? Is Jesus leading you somewhere? Is He showing you something? Or is He reminding you of something? Take time to talk to God and ask Him what is on His heart for you, what He loves about you and write what comes to mind (spare pages for notes are at the back if you need more space).

HOLDING TIGHT

#Day20

"If I rise on the wings of the dawn, if I settle on the far side of the sea, even there Your hand will guide me, Your right hand will hold me fast."

(Psalm 139:10)

What are your feelings about rollercoasters? Love them or hate them, there are different reasons why you might find them a bit scary. Some are frightening because of the sudden dips and turns they have, throwing you unexpectedly from side to side. Others are horrifying because of the heights they manage, only to dive at great speed. However, for me the most terrifying ones are those where they don't feel at all secure! I'm sure you've been on those rollercoasters where the metal bar that's supposed to keep you in only comes down so far. I remember noticing the enormous gap between me and the bar keeping me fastened to my seat. However, calling out "I'm really not comfortable with this!!!" as the car is trundling off towards the first turn is too late.

Here we see two things that we rely upon for God to help us with in this journey of life: guidance and protection. We're reading that God's hand guides us and holds us tight. Much like a rollercoaster ride, our lives can take so many unexpected turns, where events happen that shake us up, unsettle us or make us feel sick. Of course there are also the highs of love, the successes and the joys of life as well as the lows of disappointment, grief and hardship.

God is aware of the dangers that these events can have on our soul and unlike the wobbly bar of a scary rollercoaster God is actually there keeping us secure. *"Your right hand will hold me fast,"* means that God holds us tightly in His grip of protection, enabling us to bravely face those challenges with His help. Interestingly we read God's "hand" guides, but His "right hand" holds us fast. In those days, referring to the right hand had the added meaning of strength. Where we are most weak, God supplies His strength protecting those areas of our lives that are most vulnerable.

Where are you most vulnerable? Do you let fear hold you back, concerned that you'll mess it all up? Maybe you struggle to control your emotions, which gets you into bother? Perhaps you're not so self-assured and you have a tough time believing in yourself? Or it could be something else completely. We all have weaknesses and they are often highlighted more when times of pressure hit us or when we feel far away from God.

The words we read at the start reinforce the truth that God is close, helping us to navigate those problems that come our way. Whether you feel far from God or close, just know that He is a holding your life securely, on course for where He wants you to be in the future. God wants you and values you. Knowing you better than you know yourself, He is aware of those weaknesses that threaten to hold you back from His plan.

So God in His guidance and protection will help you work on those areas of challenge, in order to give you strength for living your life. He may lead you through times of testing in order to make you strong. Don't make the mistake of believing during those times that God isn't protecting you or isn't bothered about you. He will do a work within your heart that is so valuable and will lead you through it all in His timing. It won't all be difficult though! He will make things easy for you and give you rest when you need it most too.

Father God. I thank You that You provide strength for me in times when I feel I can't do it. Thank You that I am secure because You hold me tight, protecting me from giving up altogether. I thank You that you have good plans for my future and that when I trust You for today, each and every day I see you treating me favourably. Like Your favourite child! I love You!

HIDDEN FROM SEEING GOD

#Day21

"If I say "Surely the darkness will hide me and the light become night around me, even the darkness will not be dark to You;" (Psalm 139:11-12)

Once a term, there's an event in our house which is guaranteed to send our younger family members into hiding. Even the mention of this event will draw groans and protests, as if I had just announced a compulsory sprout eating contest or something! Suddenly when the time approaches I can hear a pin drop in the house and people are nowhere to be seen. They've all gone into hiding. I remember setting up to get things ready and going to the under-stairs cupboard for the vacuum cleaner, only to find someone already in there! Methinks he won't be hiding in there next time! Found you!!

Of course we're talking about haircut day; something that should only take 20 minutes, but has become a thing of larger proportions.

You know, if you think about something long enough, especially something negative that you have to deal with, it can begin to grow in your mind becoming something you dread. I'm not recommending doing this by the way! In fact the very opposite! But I'm sure you can understand those times where a test or exam looms and the more you think about it, the more you fear its negative consequences.

The Hebrew word for "hide" in this verse is also translated as "overwhelm" to read "If I say *"Surely the darkness will overwhelm me."* [a] To be overwhelmed is to be taken beyond your ability to cope. It's possible when negative thoughts have got to us that we can feel hidden away from God's reach, overwhelmed by doubt, fear or concern. It's like a cloud of darkness descends, forming a cover over our minds between us and God; trying to make us doubt that God can help. As this darkness closes in, even our attitudes can become unhealthy and we feel far from God. When this happens part of us can become numb to God, almost shying away from Him.

In listing all of the places that God will find us, the writer adds that the darkness doesn't have a secret corner from God either. It's like the Psalmist is saying "Even if I were to invite thoughts into my heart that were to overwhelm me, God You can still see my heart amongst all the darkness that hovers there." Once in, the darkness will try and hide us from seeing God during those negative moments too.

Yet God, motivated by love will break through all of this and rescue us. God is able to get to us. Quite a dark thing to say to God, really; but in saying it the Psalmist is recognising the fact that nothing can keep us from God. You can call out to Him any time, in the middle of the darkness when you're afraid or in the brightest day when things are all good. You won't be hidden from God. Darkness doesn't have the power to conceal us from God.

So I want to suggest something to you. If you ever find yourself falling into a dark moment, open the door for God to come in to rescue you. Reach out to God and give Him the opportunity to pull you up to Him. Without thinking, stop what you are doing, put on a worship song that you love and you will feel the darkness lose its power. Invite God in, and the darkness won't be able to stay. Tell those dark thoughts to be gone in Jesus' name and they will flee in an instant.

Lord Jesus, I thank You that You have broken the power of darkness over my life through Your death on the cross. Thank You that darkness has no weapon against me that You can't completely destroy. I'm sorry for the times that I have given darkness permission to my heart by the things I have thought, said and done. These things are not who I am and not what I want for my life. I turn away from these ways and ask You to set me free. Thank You that there is no power greater than Yours. I'm Yours forever!

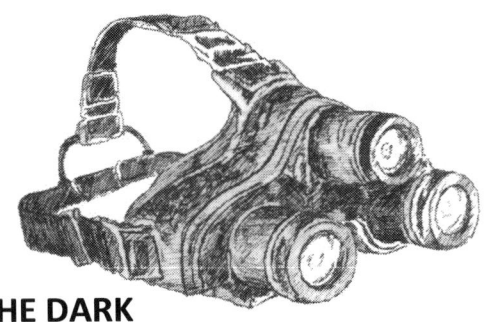

SEEING IN THE DARK

#Day22

"If I say "Surely the darkness will hide me and the light become night around me, even the darkness will not be dark to You; the night will shine like the day,"   (Psalm 139:12)

I was just thinking of the fun you could have with night vision goggles! Of course there are some cool educational things you could do. How about visiting the forest at night and sitting still for hours watching the foxes, badgers, owls as they come awake? Worth having security with you on that one though! Or you could go and look up at the stars when all the lights are out, seeing everything in so much more detail. But the use I was thinking of that sounded super exciting, was doing a Special Ops NERF game in the dark with night vision goggles!

Imagine having your mates around for a sleep over and getting up at midnight. Using minimal lighting, with friends as guards not knowing when you were going to make your attack. Just like Mission Impossible, stepping lightly to take up your position. Unseen and with the advantage of being able to see your enemy's movements, can you pick the right moment to advance and retrieve the hostage?!

The advantage is clear. When with normal eyes you can't see your hand in front of your face, with night vision goggles you can see exactly what the enemy is doing! If only we could see the plans of the enemy sometimes! We so easily walk into traps of temptation or fear that he sets for us. As we read those words *"even the darkness will not be dark to You; the night will shine like the day,"* we understand that God sees the intent of the enemy's plans.

The darkness cannot hide its motives from God; it's as plain as the light of day to God. He can see what the enemy is planning. God works against the plots the enemy has, to turn them for good.

Now you might be asking the question "Why then does God even allow evil into this world?" The answer is that we as humans invited evil in. In the book of Genesis we read about how God made the world and that everything was good. This is the way God wanted the world to be, good and without any evil. Within a beautiful and vast garden that God planted on the earth were many trees, loads that produced fruit of all kinds.

There was however one tree which God planted that produced fruit that God didn't want Adam and Eve to eat. This was the tree of the knowledge of good and evil. In fact Adam and Eve already knew what good was. The whole world with them in it was all good. The choice for them was whether they also wanted to know evil too. God was saying to them "Don't eat the fruit from this tree because if you do you will discover what evil is like. You will experience evil and invite it into this world." God wanted us to only experience what is good.

So God didn't let evil into this world. He gave us humans the choice, the free will and we (our ancestors Adam and Eve) let evil in. Of course we might say "I would have obeyed God," yet we say that knowing what evil does to the world, how it causes wars, hate, violence, abuse and misery. Now that we've experienced evil we just want the good! We want peace in this world. Thankfully God has provided such a place in the life to come, heaven; through His Son, where people have chosen just the good.

Going back to our night vision goggles, where we can see the enemy's movements, but they can't see ours! God sees what the enemy tries to achieve. Since humans invited the evil to this earth, it has a legal right to be active on this earth. Yet the plans that the enemy has for evil, God sees them and turns them for His own good and for the good of those who love Him. The darkness can't hide its ways from God, it's as obvious as being in the light to God, yet the devil is unaware of God's plans for us! God is on a mission to save us!

FINDING BEAUTY

#Day23

If I say "Surely the darkness will hide me and the light become night around me, even the darkness will not be dark to You; the night will shine like the day," for darkness is as light to You." (Psalm 139:12)

One of the most famous paintings ever created is the Mona Lisa. Instantly recognisable, I'm no expert, but it must be worth several $100 million. One year when I was in Paris with my lovely wife Debs, we were going to take a look at the Mona Lisa. Unfortunately the queues in the Louvre art gallery where it was displayed went around the block. To view it would have resulted in an hour's wait in order to glimpse it for about 20 seconds!

But why is the Mona Lisa so famous? Pardon me for saying this, but she isn't even pretty! Yet people are captivated by her smile and the atmosphere of the painting. Although she may be ugly, there is also a beauty that shines through the Mona Lisa at the same time!

So how can darkness be as light to God? Let's make sense of it… We have seen that dark thoughts can overwhelm us, but that the darkness can't hide or keep God away from us. Furthermore God sees the plans of darkness and He works on our behalf turning those situations around for our good. So darkness cannot negatively influence the way God sees. Whether the darkness covers our own minds, or makes plans for our downfall, these can't be hidden from God.

"Darkness and light are alike to You" doesn't mean that darkness is good or light is bad, or that good and evil are the same. No, none of that. It means that the darkness cannot cover what would be seen in daylight.

The darkness and ugliness inside our own hearts cannot shield God from seeing the light and beauty that He has created. He is aware of the ugliness and darkness in our hearts; but much like the Mona Lisa, God sees through all of that to capture the beauty of who He has made you and me to be. When you and I see the ugliness that is inside, it can cause us to feel shame. Yet when God sees inside our hearts He is conscious of our imperfections, yet that isn't what He chooses to see! He sees a masterpiece, a painting of value worth hundreds of millions of pounds/dollars!

I once had a dream that I was doing a painting. I was making good progress and in the dream my dad came up to me and said, "Wow. That is a lovely painting." Then he picked it up and viewed it closer, holding it up to the light. He then said to me "Do you realise there is another painting underneath this one?" I was like "What??" So I took another look at the painting and realised that there was indeed a different painting underneath mine. Yet it wasn't just any painting. It was one that had been skilfully done by a master painter. It was the sort that would hang in the most prestigious galleries of the world.

I realised at this point that I had to remove the work that I had done so that this masterpiece could be seen. I felt that God was telling me that He created me and that He had a beautiful work and plan for my life. He knew what good things He had placed inside of me that He wanted to draw out for all to see.

All things are visible to God. The failures that make us feel bad about ourselves are not the first things He sees when He looks at you and me. He sees a beautiful person whom He dearly loves and the masterpiece He is making you and me to be.

Father God. I thank You that you see me, warts and all and that you love me just the same. I thank You that you have made me beautiful and have chosen me to be your masterpiece. I will not call ugly what You have made beautiful. In Jesus' name!

FROM THE INSIDE OUT

#Day24

"For You created my inmost being;"   (Psalm 139:13)

Some years ago there was an all-girl pop group called the Spice Girls that took the world by storm. Their first song "Wannabe" was such a hit that it was the biggest selling debut single of all time. I remember each singer dressed in a certain way. Posh spice always had the fashionable look and Sporty spice wore tracksuit bottoms and a Liverpool football top. Ginger spice was so called because of her vibrant hair. Baby spice went for the cute look and Scary spice... well I don't know about her, she certainly wasn't in a Frankenstein outfit or anything. Each one had their own look to communicate an identity to their fans, which they would then have to live up to. But what if one day Posh spice wanted to go to the shops in her jogging outfit? Or Ginger spice wanted to go blonde?

Sometimes we can associate with a particular group or label, be it Goths, Emos or Nerds and feel we have to dress in a certain way to live up to that label. Yet our identity actually starts from the inside out rather than the outside in. It's not what you look like on the outside that should shape who you are. Our identity is found in so much more than our appearance, group membership, or affiliation to a particular organisation. God has formed character on the inside of us, rather than a popular image to live up to. A person can sometimes catch a glimpse of what we are like by gazing into our eyes, but to really know who a person is takes time and is discovered through the ups and downs of life.

How can we discover our identity? You might be asking the question, "Who am I really on the inside? Am I trying to live up to an image I have created of myself; one that just doesn't fit who I really am? We can do this can't we? You know, we'll act all tough when we're out with our mates, but then we're different where there's less pressure to be part of the in crowd. Perhaps there are some places where there's more space to be yourself? God has established who you are from those things inside of you; your personality, the way you approach life, the quality of your character. Maybe you're a loyal friend, or you're someone who doesn't give up easily. Perhaps you are a strong willed individual or see the world in a positive light and are very optimistic. Other character traits such as being an encourager, a leader or an arty type all make up who you might be on the inside.

It's likely that you will come up against challenging situations where you feel pulled into being someone that you are not. Maybe you have a really good caring heart, but when you're with some people you end up gossiping or criticising others behind their backs. There's something deeper inside that makes us who we are. It's complex and put together by God. Much like an onion, that if you peeled away the layers which form as you grow up, you would discover the truth about who you are; not who the world wants you to be, but who God Himself made you to be.

Our inmost being has been created by God. If you have ever bought an item of tech, particularly one you are unfamiliar with; you'll be asking the question, "How do I work this thing?" For that we need the user manual. We need to go to the one who made us. Since He put us together from the very core; that bit that can't be seen, *"You created my inmost being."*

So the question is, what does God say about who you are? You are unique. Skilfully made and particularly designed to become a friend of God. Your life has meaning, your thoughts are precious and your love is greatly sought after by God.

Father God. I thank You that You want me. I know You were calling out to me, before I even knew who You were. You were there, leaving clues for me to find You because You wanted me, because You made me and I am Yours. Thank You that You still want me. Thank You that I find more about who I am by discovering more of what You are like, because I am made in Your image. In Jesus' name. (PTO)

71

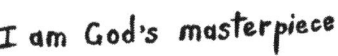

I am valued
Matt 10:30-31

I am like an arrow in God's hand

Psalm 127:3-4

I am God's masterpiece

God's breath is in me

John 14:15-17

Ephesians 2:10

I am one of God's children

I am God's creation

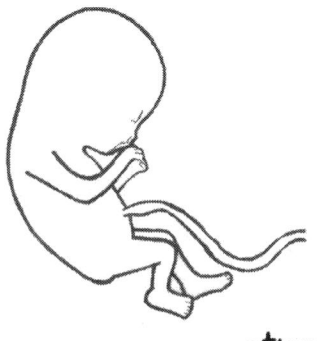

I am a Friend of God

John 15:15

I am a new creation
2 Corinthians 5:7

PRAYER SPACE

Take a look at these inside traits. Circle which ones describe you...

big personality

lively

enthusiastic

bright

brave

imginative

team player

adveturous

inventive

skilful

active

arty

Practical

perseverer

determined

creative

strong willed

understanding

caring

thoughtful

approachable

quick witted

reliable

sociable

visionary

thinker

dreamer

good humoured

73

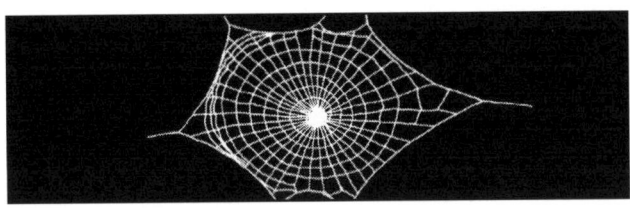

ORIGINS

#Day25
"For You created my inmost being," (Psalm 139:13)

I'm quite into superhero films at the moment. A key part of super hero storytelling is describing the bit before the hero became super. Seeing the origins of that character's life, of how they gained their super powers is a meaningful part of the story. To watch this hard-working lad called Peter Parker suffer at the hands of a bully and face his challenges helps us to relate to the Spiderman he becomes. Knowing how it all begins gives an insight into why our hero is like he or she is now.

When you place an ordinary person into an extraordinary superhero, it brings about an interesting dynamic. In these stories we discover that "character" becomes the deciding factor between victory and defeat of these supervillains. Rather than simply using their superpowers, it's their inventiveness, past experience and resolve to do the right thing that will enable them to win. They have to dig deep inside to want to fight in the face of great danger! Obviously Spiderman is a made up story and there are plenty of real heroes who didn't plan to be heroic; yet something was placed in their DNA that made them rise to the emerging challenge.

Our origins are what make us who we are today. Our beginning shapes what passions might become important to us in the future. Maybe you have the heart of a warrior or a protector? Perhaps you are naturally motivated about impacting the lives of others for good? As we take another look at this verse it literally means "You Yourself created my kidneys"! The writer is talking about a place deep inside that is unseen, deep in your soul. We could describe it a bit like your conscience.

Our conscience (much like a spider-sense) alerts us when we're about to do something wrong. Suddenly, eating that piece of cake that your mum told you not to take is not so enjoyable! Our conscience is a very helpful guide.   Yet some think that their conscience is all they need for understanding their identity.   Unfortunately our thoughts can't always be relied upon, because telling the difference between our conscience and our feelings can be tricky! It's easy for a criminal to say "This is the way I feel God has made me, so I'm going to steal stuff" and be very wrong about it!

Yesterday we said that it's from the inside out that we discover who we are. You might be wondering to yourself "What are my origins?" First and foremost your origins start with God, since He created you, body, soul and spirit. Those who look to answer key questions about themselves without first seeking out the wisdom of God as found in the whole Bible can easily become unstuck. It's like buying a new piece of tech, but ignoring the maker's instruction manual on how to work it.

How do I find God's purpose for my life? To discover clues about God's mission for your life it's worth asking, "What is God revealing to me about my life?" And "What stirs my soul?" The origins of God's calling have been put deep inside you since before day one! What desires spur you on or fire you up? What Bible verses light up your heart? Maybe you've always got a melody going round in your head and music is your thing? Could it be you're a talker and you love interacting with people? Perhaps you dream of adventure and are a bit of a risk taker? There's an inner motivation that God placed inside each one of us when He made us. Much like our conscience it's often something we become aware of when we're faced with options, helping us to choose. God also loves to confirm His ways in a concrete way as you read His word. Something will jump out when you least expect it as the Holy Spirit connects it with your heart. Those words on a page can become undeniable proof of God's wishes.

We've already understood that God goes behind us and before us, working out His purposes anyway. He also loves to drop clues for us to find about His plans, some are hidden deep inside waiting to be unlocked at the right time. Other clues are ready to be revealed for those who seek God and His kingdom first.

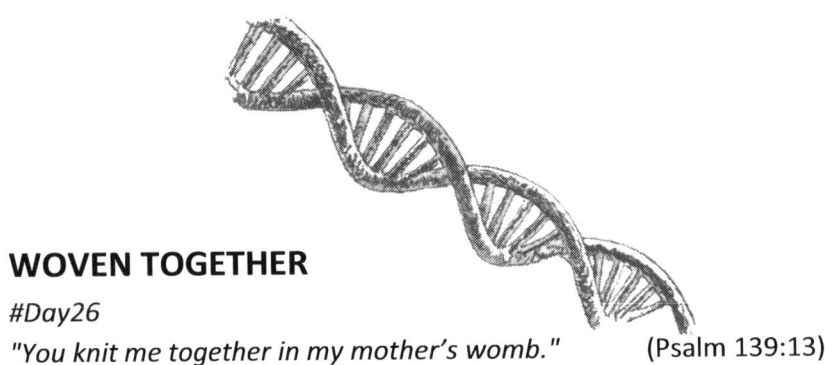

WOVEN TOGETHER

#Day26

"You knit me together in my mother's womb." (Psalm 139:13)

Did you know that identical twins aren't actually identical?? Really?? Yes Really!! They have different fingerprints! The features of every human being are shaped according to the building blocks of life, your DNA. This DNA is like a unique book written only for you, which stores the codes that instruct your cells how to form your ears, bone structure, size, personality and much more besides.

Some people say that all life was formed by random events, evolving accidentally from nothing; and because things took such a long time to come about they happened into the beautiful design we have today. I have a problem with this! Let me tell you why. In our shops and online, there are millions and millions of books that you could possibly read. Yet not one of them came about from random nothingness, not one of them was formed without an author to write them.

Take for example the binary code that you saw pictured on *#Day11*. There's actually a hidden message left in there for you to find! If you were to type in that entire binary code into an online translator [a] typing from left to right, you'll discover the message. However if you were to type them in from right to left, top to bottom, bottom to top, or another way, what you will get is going to be random nonsense. It would continue to be random nonsense unless an author was to rearrange it!

God Himself intentionally created you by writing your DNA. *"You knit me together in my mother's womb."* We understand the word knit. The original Hebrew uses the word "wove" as in how clothes were made then. In those days people would spin a thread from animal hair, then using looms, weave the threads together to make cloths. These cloths would then be sown to make clothing. In the same way God wove you together as your body formed. All of those intricate cells (like fibres in a woven fabric) are instructed by your unique DNA put there by God to form you together.

Yet our form is more than just a body. Every human has a body, soul and spirit (Hebrews 4:12). The body we have interacts in this physical world, playing football, eating breakfast, sleeping, and releasing a fart in a lift, things like that. Entwined into those experiences is our soul, which thinks and feels emotions such as the joy of hearing the school bell, or considers whether a friendship with someone will one day develop into true love. The spirit part of us connects us with God's realm, enabling us to communicate with God on a deep level (which we call prayer!). Our soul and spirit are both seamlessly interwoven into the fabric of our body by God as it develops within the womb.

How does God know you so well? Before you came into this world, God was there weaving you together inside and out. He knew what would interest you and what you would be good at today, because He knit those things into the fabric of your being. He wrote your DNA book. You have a history with God where He knew you before you even were. God even cares for the unborn! You are not an accident and don't let anyone tell you otherwise!! You were intentionally made by God and He has plan for your life which He is guiding you through even today. As His creation, God is proud of you and you are valuable to Him.

Father God. I realise how intricately you have made me, how You remember forming me and the way you have written my DNA. Thank You that You have a reason and purpose for my life according to the unique combination of features that you have given my personality. Thank You for the talents and abilities that You have given me too. As I choose to develop these, would You cause them all to improve as I use them for Your glory. In Jesus' name!

BEING ME

#Day27

"I praise You because I am fearfully and wonderfully made;"

(Psalm 139:14)

I remember in our younger days, my brothers and I were football (soccer) mad! I guess it started for me in 1982 when the World Cup was in Spain, with England scoring against France in the first 27 seconds of the game. Every time we went into the local shop to buy something, they would give us large football cards with various pictures of the players from the World Cup teams, which we then cut out and placed into an official album.

At every opportunity we would be outside playing football, with a garage door for a goal as we played on the gravel. There was always one important decision we had to make before we started the game. Who was going to be which player? Occasionally as goal keeper I was Peter Shilton. I was quite small and he was only 6ft, which lost on Top Trumps playing cards most of the time. Obviously there were more outfield players to choose from. Maybe you have heard of Diego Maradona? Four years later there was a big reason why we didn't want to be him! You could choose anyone, so Brazilian players were also popular for showing off any skills. I still do this today, "I want to be Lionel Messi!"

You know it's possible in life to actually want to be someone else; maybe because we admire them, or just wish we were like them. If someone is popular or well liked, it's easy to think we would be a better version of our self if we changed to become more like them. Of course we can learn from other people's styles to become more stylish ourselves. I remember when I had hair, going into a hairdresser's shop and asking for a Nick Faldo haircut (he was a famous golfer). There are some things we can change about our look that help as we're trying to figure out our fashion sense.

But what about those things we can't change? I remember staring at my nose in the mirror, hating how large it was. It took a while, but the rest of my face did eventually catch up. We read the words *"I praise You because I am fearfully and wonderfully made."* I know it might not always feel like that when your chin looks too pointy, your legs are all stick like or your bum has the appearance of an oversized melon. However, it's important to remember that your body is in transition where you have finished with being a child and are well on the way to being an adult.

Yet when we're not happy with our self, it's because we look at others comparing ourselves unfairly and wishing we were someone else instead. Everyone is made differently and will naturally be more blessed in some ways than others. That includes you! It's really important to appreciate that you have been wonderfully made, by someone who knows what He is doing. Some people read the word "wonderfully" and reject it, thinking it means "perfectly." Every one of us has imperfections. Perfect is a very high standard that we can sometimes set for ourselves, yet is a goal none of us will actually attain. Being human, you and I are wonderful, not perfect! We have been born into a fallen world, one of decay which takes its toll on all of God's creation.

So it's about time to accept who you are and appreciate that there's lots of amazing things about you with more good things to come. Start "being you," rather than aiming for the perfection that you believe you see in others. That's often just an illusion. God deliberately made you the way He did for a reason and discovery of these ways will come in time. You are unique and you bring something with you that no one else has. Allow God to work good things in you by taking the time to talk to Him. He will further guide you into what "being you" is all about.

Father God. I ask You to show me what You love about me. I want to discover what "being me" is all about; rather than trying to change who I am to be like others. I know that I have been made in Your image. Thank You that the only changes that I need are the ones You want to work in me. In Jesus' name!

GOD'S WORKMANSHIP

"I praise You that I am fearfully and wonderfully made.
Your works are wonderful, I know that full well." (Psalm 139:14)

There was a shop in the shopping mall where I used to live which was impossible to pass by when my boys were little. It was the clock shop. We must have been in there to get a replacement watch strap or something and whilst were waiting, took a look at the clocks. There were several wall clocks hung at an inviting height for a child displaying the words "press here." One press suddenly brought the clock to life with moving parts and music from film and TV. It was a wonder to behold.

To me the wind-up clock is such an amazing invention, designed with incredible detail and crafted so skilfully, aligned and working precisely together. Each cog turns effortlessly, supporting and turning the next. There is no part taking all of the strain, every element being important to the overall purpose of the clock.

When we think about God's works, we remember that we are part of the wider family of God, the church. God's wonderful works can be seen as we put to use our talents in partnership with God's people to help those around us. God takes what we give back to Him and brings about something wonderful through it. It's easy to read Psalm 139 and think that this life is just all about me and God and my own little world. Yet God has made you and me for a wider purpose. It says this in the Bible *"For we are God's workmanship, created in Christ Jesus for good works, which God prepared beforehand so that we would walk in them"* Ephesians 2:10.

In today's verse *"Your works are wonderful,"* hints at how we have been prepared by God beforehand, for all we will do in the future. His plans that are ahead of you somehow fit with the way He originally formed you; whether that's being a sports person, a writer, designer, an inventor, paramedic, youth worker or any combination of things. Somewhere inside you have the abilities that will one day be unlocked to fit those plans! It's all through His work and His design, all timed wonderfully to perfection.

So if you hope to one day be the scientist that achieves an amazing breakthrough, how do you make it happen? Well, think of the least strenuous form of activity that people do... Probably walking? We just read that God has prepared us beforehand so that we would <u>walk</u> in God's ways. Does that take the pressure off a bit? We are to take each day a step at a time involving God all the way, rather than working out a route to our goals and forcing things to happen. As we live out a close relationship with God, we'll see what needs to happen as those opportunities appear. Hard work is a part of that, but making a pathway to your chosen career is best done trusting the One who made you.

Much like a clock where everything depends on precision timing, God is able to make us ready for His plans when needed. Sometimes it's difficult to see this in the mess and busyness of life, when faced with unknown circumstances that appear so confusing. It can put a strain on us, where the responsible part of us says we have to have it all figured out. Yet if you were to remember the last time you walked anywhere significant, it was all about putting one step in front of the other. Just focussing on the next step rather than the next 200 will enable you to better see God's working and His timing in the events that affect us.

We're meant to let God take the strain! God sets us in motion and like a part of a watch we do our thing in connection with the rest of God's people. You are an essential cog in the workings of God. As a baby in your mother's womb God was designing and considering your future. He was fitting you together not in isolation, but with others in mind that you would one day meet and He is still doing this today! Talk about a wonderful God!

Why not listen to a worship song and write what comes to mind... (PTO)

GOD YOU ARE WONDERFUL

Things I adore about You

Things about You that make me happy

Reasons why I worship You

Things I am in awe of

Things You are brilliant at God

Songs I want to sing to You

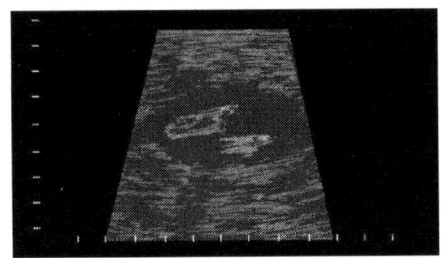

SACRED

#Day29

"My frame was not hidden from You when I was made in the secret place, when I was woven together in the depths of the earth"   (Psalm 139:15)

I remember the day my wife and I went for the ultra-sound scan for our first baby. It was an exciting moment where we were going to catch a glimpse of the wee fella for the first time! Up to that point, we had talked to him, played music to him, but that was about it. As we watched the TV screen we saw a black and white image with what looked like a small potato on it and we were like, "wait, what are we seeing?" The nurse then confirmed that it wasn't indeed a potato, but our first born child, in his early stages. The scan that I sketched out above was the wee man at 20 weeks, and yes those are his feet!

Obviously it's difficult to see clearly on an ultra-sound scan, but it's important to say that this is the place where life has already started. Although it's a hidden place of secret, unseen by human eyes; it's where we begin our journey of life. Even in here we are important and draw the attention of God.

We read the words *"My frame was not hidden from You when I was made in the secret place, when I was woven together in the depths of the earth."* The thought might come to mind, "Doesn't the writer know how babies are made?? They don't come from the depths of the earth!!" What He's doing here is using picture language to communicate the concept of life originating in a deep place; with it being more than just a location, but linking it to creation. It reminds me of the language found in Genesis 1:2 *"The earth was without form and void, and darkness was over the face of the deep. And the Spirit of God was hovering over the face of the waters."* He's describing the sacred moment of the creation of a new life. It's sacred because it is something cherished, precious where God is involved, it's utterly priceless and to be preserved at all costs.

It's quite a shock to the system, the moment you are responsible for making decisions for a life other than your own. I remember a friend of mine who was a dad, saying "Becoming a father will change you forever." Once it's there within the womb however small or unseen, in partnership with Creator God, a new person has been brought into this world. It is at least as important as your own life, to be protected as precious. For me, my children's lives are even more important than my own and I would give mine up to keep theirs safe.

There's a lot said about people's views when it comes to the life of the unborn child and people's rights. Yet whatever people say, it's obvious from what we've been reading that our lives are sacred, beautifully crafted and cherished. How can God create something so precious and beautiful, for us to throw it away? So what happens then to those who don't even get a chance of life? It's clear that we are not hidden from God. We are formed by God, known by Him and as unborn children we are of great value to Him. I believe the unborn who don't make it, will be with Him in eternity.

In this world God's creation is still continuing. Scientists tell us that space is still expanding. You and I are a part of this, created by God as valuable, with a purpose and equipped to fulfil it. God intended to make you, just as He intended to create the earth. You are not just another human, not just a number amongst millions, you are precious to God.

Father God. I thank You that no part of my life is hidden from You. From the very first moment that I existed, to this moment and beyond I feel Your involvement and Your love. Thank You that even if I was in a crowded stadium of a 100,000 people, You wouldn't miss what was going on in my heart. I'm never hidden from You or far from Your thoughts. I know that You made me for a reason. May my life go down in the history of creation as someone who significantly influenced others for good. In Jesus' name!

FORMED BY GOD

"Your eyes saw my unformed body;" (Psalm 139:16)

I remember in art being given the chance to do some pottery on a wheel. At the time I turned it down because I didn't want to get all messy and I couldn't see the point in making a pot. Nowadays I've changed a bit and have realised that art and mess pretty much go together. Wouldn't it be great to try and make something useful like a mug that would become your favourite for a cuppa? Maybe you would craft a cereal bowl? What about a super cool lampshade for a table lamp in your room? Oh the possibilities are endless!

It's exciting starting something new, a clean slate or a blank page. I love the thrill of being inspired with the potential of what I'm going to make. Of course there can be those moments when the blank page stares back at me and the ideas are lacking; but when I have a design and the ideas are flowing, I can be pretty unstoppable!

We see the words *"Your eyes saw my unformed body"* and like a potter viewing a piece of clay, God views you and senses the vast possibilities for your life. With an idea in His mind, God looked at you and me in our embryonic state and lovingly began to form us.

Why are you wonderful? Because you have been created by God and designed to His specifications. You have been formed according to the plan of the One who cares deeply for you from the moment He set His eyes on you. You were designed by God in a moment of inspiration and loved by Him. That should make you pretty unstoppable!

For those of you who are *Lord of the Rings* fans, the Hebrew word for embryo is pronounced *"gōlem"*! You are definitely God's precious!! (He's obviously nothing like Gollum though). As an embryo you would think God might say "Oh there's nothing much going on here yet, I'll come back in a couple of weeks." Yet even in such a basic state, we draw the loving attentions of our Heavenly Father. When there's nothing even going on, He's interested in us! Can you imagine the delight that was in God's heart when He saw you for the first time?!! As He looked He saw a vision of what could be for your life. He doesn't give up at that point either.

We've been reading about not being able to get away from God even if we tried. He's constantly working in our lives, going before us, searching our hearts to see where we're at, watching our backs and guiding us. We are being pointed towards our potential, something which is up to us to take a hold of.

On a potter's wheel, the clay has to be wetted and soft. If it has been left out on a window sill it will dry out, becoming solid and impossible to manage. If the potter were to try and mould it in its hardened form it would just crack and crumble. Much like dried out clay (if we wanted to), it's possible for you and me to harden our hearts to God. When He attempts to shape you by presenting you with a challenge or opportunity, do you welcome it or resist it? When you are faced with doing wrong, knowing what God says is right, do you submit to God's way of doing things or choose your own way? God's full potential is released when we work in partnership with His shaping of our lives.

As God saw you for the first time, with the length of your life in view, He created someone wonderful. He won't reveal it all to you as a blueprint all at once though. As your life progresses, God will begin to unravel His plans for you, telling you His promises for your life and confirming His work in you. In the highs and lows of life, in successes and mistakes He remains with you unfolding your potential.

Father God. As the clay for the potter, I submit to You as you shape my life. I trust that in all things You know best. In Jesus' name!

NOT ROBOTS

#Day31

"all the days ordained for me were written in Your book
before one of them came to be."   (Psalm 139:16)

Imagine you're in a world where your entire life is scheduled, pre-planned by someone else. We'll call them a life planner, where what you wear, when you eat, how much exercise you do is all decided for you. Maybe life might feel a little restricted, especially if you want to be out with friends. Add to the schedule exact bed times and limits on how long you are allowed in the shower and even on the toilet! Sounds a bit like the army or something! Feeling a little controlled yet? What if that person then mapped out how you can spend your free time, ensuring you have a healthy balance of worthwhile pursuits? Is it sounding scary yet! Or is that just a normal day for you?! If that is you, I'm guessing you're the President of the United States!

Some people think that our lives are controlled by God like robots that are unable to freely decide for themselves. I get a little nervous when people say the words "God is in control." I understand what people mean, that there is no situation that God can't cope with. God is King of the Universe and as King, when He speaks a decree it will happen. Yet God has also handed to us humans the controls to our lives. We call this free will, the ability to choose to go God's way or our own. Adam and Eve made their choice and it was against God's will. God is not a control freak!

At first glance the words *"all the days ordained for me were written in Your book before one of them came to be"* appear to say the opposite! Is everything really destined to happen with nothing we can do to change it?

As God sees us in embryonic form, He sees our days. He is somehow outside of time, observing the span of our lives before even a day has begun. It's at this point He chooses to influence our lives, adding the creativity of a master potter, shaping what is to come. Rather than the idea of being controlled, the word *ordained* here uses that picture of the potter that we looked at yesterday. God crafts into your DNA the person you will be, like an instruction book with information on who you are. As you take your place in this generation you begin a new record of heaven's exploits on earth, fulfilling your role in God's plan.

So is God in control or not? Well, there's a tension between God's rule and human freedom. In the Bible there are a couple of key Greek words that are used for God's will. One of them *boulomai* is used to mean the deliberate plan of God that He has decided on that cannot be changed. The other word for God's will *thelema* is less strong and is more like a wish or desire which humans can reject. We know that it's God's wish that all people are saved from an eternity without Him, yet sadly that's a desire which we know that some people will reject.

On the other hand no one could change God's plan to save us, not Herod killing the babies after Jesus' birth, not the devil tempting Jesus, or those who tried to fling Jesus off a cliff.

So there are some things that God desires for our lives that are dependent on our actions. We know that when we pray God answers where if we didn't pray He might not! Acting obediently according to His will sees results that otherwise wouldn't occur. Yet regarding God's unchanging will, if He were to plan an event to take place in our lives such as inventing a cure for cancer; nothing would be able to prevent it from happening.

So we are not robots, pre-programmed or restricted, unable to make real choices for ourselves. We can (unwisely) choose to reject God's ways, but who would want to turn down His loving acts of kindness to us! There will be times when God sees fit to intervene on our behalf according to His will, which He can do because He is God; the master potter!

Father God. I give you my life willingly. I know this means that you require my obedience. Please guide me and lead me. I will follow! In Jesus' name!

PRECIOUS THOUGHTS

#Day32

"How precious to me are Your thoughts, God!"   (Psalm 139:17)

Some time ago I felt God wanted me to mix things up a little during a Monday night youth group session. I was speaking to teenagers about how God loves to talk to us. Towards the end of the session, I asked if anyone would like God to speak to them? Most of those in the room didn't believe in God, but all were happy to give it a go. I numbered some pieces of paper (one for each person), folding them up before randomly giving them out. Everyone had a different number which they were not to reveal. I would then say one of the numbers given out and tell what I felt God loved about that person.

We prayed and as I suggested a number to start, a picture came into my head. As I explained what I felt God was saying, more thoughts came. I continued calling numbers out, saying the good things God saw in that person; when I began to notice some of the group giggling amongst themselves. Not wanting to spoil the vibe, I just continued as they seemed to be enjoying it! It turned out that they had secretly shown each other their numbers. What they found hilarious was the accuracy of the things I was telling them about that person. I clearly had no idea which of them I was talking to, but they knew and realised it could only be God!

"How precious to me are Your thoughts, God!" is the writer exclaiming, "How amazing it is to discover what God sees!" To be told the information God knows about us is something worth finding out! We all need encouragement about our identity when we're feeling low in confidence, or uncertain about the future. Words like these are precious because of the power and truth they hold. They give us the will to keep going when

it's tough because we understand a bit more about why we are here. As God speaks His words into your heart, you'll have an inner peace about those things that concern you and maybe even have a sense of His calling for your life. In comparison to some of the things that people value, knowing how God sees you is a million times better!

Maybe you are thinking that you'd like God to speak to you? You are no different from me. You have the same Holy Spirit inside you whom Jesus says *"He will guide you into all truth"* (John 16:13). He (the Holy Spirit) will tell you what Jesus knows. I didn't have any earth shattering spiritual experience to hear from God. I wasn't struck by lightning in a lively service or ended up stuck to the floor, nothing incredible like that! Of course I have received the Holy Spirit, been prayed for often and sought God that He would speak to me more. This is something you can do too!

How then do I hear God's thoughts? I've found that it begins by learning whether something might be God or not, through reading the Bible. I have a small artist's sketchbook which I value very highly, because it has become my prayer journal. A journal is a bit like a diary, where you write down thoughts; but a prayer journal is different as it contains thoughts from God. Every time I feel God is speaking to me in a special way, I write it in my journal. It could be that I'm reading a Bible verse and suddenly I realise God is telling me something special through it. This journal is full of pictures that have come to mind when God was guiding me in some way and I sketched them out. When I listen to someone talk from the Bible and am inspired it goes in the journal, as do any dreams I have that tell a story.

I believe that as we record down God's words that are precious to us, He sees how much we value them; this makes Him want to show us more!

Father God. I think it is amazing that You want to talk to me! Help me to understand the ways that You like to communicate with me. I commit to seeking after You and spending more time reading Your word in order to know what You are saying to me. Come Holy Spirit. Please speak and show me more of Jesus and Father God!

Jesus,
What do you love about me?

I want to know Your heart

Ask the Holy Spirit to ignite
a passion for Jesus in your heart

Holy Spirit
Please remind
me what Jesus
is like...

THINKING OF YOU

#Day33

*"How precious to me are Your thoughts God! How vast the sum of them!
Were I to count them, they would outnumber the grains of sand."*

(Psalm 139:17)

Today our go to place for information is Google. I use it all the time to learn things that would otherwise take me hours to figure out on my own. If I want to fix something on my car, Google will lead me to a video showing me step by step how it's done. Maybe I want to learn a new skill like doing trick shots with a Yo-Yo, or be able to speak fluently in a new language. Google will even enable me to do a virtual walk down the Champs-Élysées towards the Arc de Triomphe, finding places to eat before visiting Paris for real. As a search engine, we tell it what we need and it then provides options in order to direct us to the required solution. Such knowledge is super handy to have access to if you ask it the right questions.

However, what if you don't know what to ask? Or if the solution given is to visit a doctor, to talk to someone, or to be brave? Suddenly we realise that although search engines are handy, they are no replacement for our need for God to be with us, personally present, understanding where we're at and working on our behalf.

The bit we're reading now, *"How precious to me are Your thoughts God! How vast the sum of them! Were I to count them, they would outnumber the grains of sand"* is summing up all that has been said so far. God has searched our thoughts and seen our ways. He understands our motivations and can tell what we are going to say before we say it. God is close, aware of where we are located, guiding us and keeping us secure. Even when we feel hidden from Him and lost, He is close. He was there at our beginning. He knows the origins of our lives up to this point and sees how things will pan out in the days to come. So when He reveals His thoughts about you, He really knows what He's talking about! If He were on a Mastermind quiz show, you would be His specialised subject!

It's in moments when we feel weak that God wants to remind us that He is close and understands every detail of what we're going through. He has the strength that we need in order to be brave. He sees the great things about us when we're minded to put ourselves down or miss the significance of who we are. God is aware of all that complex stuff that goes on through our minds and He can lead us to talk to someone, giving them the wisdom we need for that moment.

I'm sure when you've sat on a beach you have never attempted to count the grains of sand. Even trying to count a handful would take some considerable time. God's thoughts outnumber the sand, not a handful or a bucket load or even just one beach! We're talking about more than a whole coast line! And do you know the most amazing thing?? All of these thoughts, countless as they are, they are all about you. It says *"How precious to me…"* but it also can mean *"How precious **concerning me** are Your thoughts God."* "Okay Paul," you say, "aren't you over-egging this grain of sand thing? That is way too many thoughts to be just about me." I don't think so. He has numbered the hairs on your head! (Matthew 10:30). These are not just random thoughts either or useless facts! They are deep thoughts within the mind of God toward you, because He is concerned for your welfare and is working for Your good.

So as you invite God into your world, you can step confidently knowing that you are not in this alone. You can call to your loving Father God for help and as the best dad ever He is there with you. He believes in you, because He created you and knows how great you are!

Father God. I thank You that You are always with me. Thank You that You are always thinking of me with countless thoughts concerning me. Thank You that You love to make Your vast resources available to me when I'm searching for help. Even if all I need is someone to be with me, I know that You are here. I love You. In Jesus' name.

THE GOODNESS OF GOD

#Day34

"When I awake, I am still with You."　　　　(Psalm 139:18)

If you have a busy life, I'm sure you can appreciate the morning rush to get in to school or wherever you need to be that day. With loads of things to remember, getting ready can be a stressful time of day. Suddenly thoughts crowd in to your mind. Have you packed all the right stuff for that day? PE kit? Got your lunch? Your bus pass? Is it exam season and you need a special timetable? What about your phone? Are you on time? Did you remember to brush your teeth?? Forgetting any of it can be a source of great stress and threaten to bring your hopes for a good day to a grinding halt. It's easy for panic to set in when faced with the consequences of failing to put your homework in your bag. Keep your chin up. It will be okay.

So here's a question... Do you start your day with God? Do you invite Him into your day? The words, *"When I awake, I am still with You,"* talk about this very thing. Obviously after all we have read in the Psalm, we know that God is with us waking or sleeping; but what I'm asking is this: at the very start of the day, when you open your eyes, do you acknowledge Jesus is there? It's easy to wake up and have a million thoughts come crashing into your mind. What you have to do, where you have to be, who you've got to see and things you might need to say. We've seen that God knows all of that, every bit. It's already passed through His mind. He has it taken care of already as you welcome Him in at the start of your day. You don't necessarily have to list all your worries to Him. It might help to tell Him any big ones, but just being with Him at the start invites His favour.

See, God is good. He loves to provide for us, especially in those moments where we are unprepared for what is coming next. It's easy for something to go pear-shaped and cause us a large amount of stress. Yet God goes before us and behind us, so having Him on board is worth it!

Just the other day I was dropping off Henry at school. There's this drop off point for cars where they are meant to do just that, drop someone off and drive away. Well it was full up with parked cars, so I drove further and parked the car in the car park. As I walked Henry to the school gate, the thought popped into my head to ask, "Do you know what class you are in today?" Most of his class were away on a school trip and he had been joining random classes during the week. He looked at me blankly and said he couldn't remember. Suddenly I was glad that I hadn't just dropped him off and gone. He would have been left wandering around for some time unable to get into his locked classroom. I took him to the school reception and he was all sorted!

I love it when God does things like this! Who'd have thought cars parked in the drop off zone would be a blessing?! He makes a way for us that we didn't know we needed. God's thoughts are as vast as the sand on the sea shore. He has processed all of the things we could ever worry about. I love to notice when He provides the solutions for those problems before they even come to my attention. When we invite God into our day, it's like we are teaming up with Him and He just loves to provide for us in ways like this.

When you wake up, God is there with you. He can fill in all of the gaps in your day that you aren't able to do. It's easy to be distracted by stuff that you weren't expecting to happen and then make mistakes or get stressed. You have God the Almighty with you. Maybe He wants to tell you something as you start your day. It could be an encouragement about who you are, so that you walk in to school with confidence. It could be He wants you to encourage someone else, or He wants to draw worship out of you, so that you can feel Him close throughout the day.

Father God. I invite You into my day. Please take care of the things that I cannot do. I thank You that You go ahead of me and provide for me in unexpected ways. Every time I notice You doing this I'll thank You!!

FACING THE CHALLENGE

#Day35

"If only You, God, would slay the wicked! Away from me, you who are bloodthirsty!" (Psalm 139:19)

I remember there being some elements of school that I really disliked; cross country running in the cold was one of them and class detentions another. My class was often very rowdy with a few individuals annoying the teacher enough to bring punishment upon the whole class. There was no justice! Then there was Chemistry. A subject I hated because people who shouldn't be allowed within 5 metres of a knife and fork were given free access to experiment with hazardous chemicals and Bunsen burners.

Yet there was one even less enjoyable aspect of school life, the troublemakers. You know the kind I'm talking about. When they are around trouble is not far behind. I'm sure you know the type I mean. They are aggressive, selfish, unkind and always seem to be in conflict with someone. They could start an argument in an empty room. Now it wouldn't be so bad if the conflicts they had were with people as equally as unpleasant. They could rage against each other and leave the rest of us alone! Unfortunately that rarely happened in my time at school. It was often the innocent who were targeted, those who were different, who were good or who worked hard (the least likely to fight back).

I expect you have experienced something similar and like the Psalm writer you just want to say "go away you nasty bloodthirsty people!!" They come at you with accusations, making up an argument to justify their aggression in their own eyes; but it's all lies.

You have the potential inside you for great things, but this potential will be challenged. We talked earlier on in this book about the potential that

God is looking for in you and how He wants to draw that out. There is also an enemy who wants to destroy that potential. This enemy is jealous of God's creation and doesn't want God's goodness to shine out. What is the best way to stop someone from doing what they are best at? It's to discourage that person. If we are led to believe the nasty lies that people say about us or our talents, we can feel like giving up. When they put down our achievements or say our efforts are not worth it, it leads us to question our worth because it's an attack on who we are.

Great potential does not go unchallenged!! The amazing things that God wants to do in you start small and grow in strength and significance. Whilst these things are developing, it will take perseverance on your part with God's help to keep going with it. When people put us down it's easy to start comparing ourselves with others. Unfortunately comparison is the thief of joy. The excitement that you have doing the things you are good at can disappear when thoughts like "I'll never be as good as..." come to mind. You are in a developmental stage where (like me) you have no idea what wonderful potential God is going to draw out of you.

I would say I'm quite a late developer. At school (apart from English and art), my grades were very average. Yet now at the age of ummm... over 40 I can see that God has given me so many wonderful talents. So don't ever give up!! You have God given potential in you, so persevere through this hardship and see how God will bring to life all of your potential!

False accusations are hard to take, so remember who you are! You are sons and daughters in God's kingdom. You are loved by God, known by Him and He is always close by. Don't be afraid. Keep going because you have an unstoppable God with you who goes before and behind you!

Father God. I want to thank You that You have placed so much potential in me. I reject the lies of those who would say otherwise. You know me and You know the truth about me. Help me to rise to the challenge that I am faced with and to persevere with the talents that You have given me. In Jesus' name!

WAR

#Day36

"They speak of You with evil intent; Your adversaries misuse Your name. Do I not hate those who hate You, LORD, and abhor those who are in rebellion against You? I have nothing but hatred for them; I count them my enemies." (Psalm 139:20-22)

Whilst I was studying at Bible College during the late 1990s I had the most intense dream. I know what you are going to ask next, and no it wasn't during a lesson! In this dream it was like I had woken up in the middle of a war zone. I'm sure if you've seen those films like *Dunkirk* or *Saving Private Ryan* you can imagine the sort of setting I'm describing. In my dream the sky was dark, planes were flying overhead and in the distance I could see the trenches of the front line. It was a war zone.

As I took in the scene I saw what seemed to be a factory production line in progress with a long conveyor belt. In the centre of all that was going on a person was supervising everything (like a Nazi officer), demanding that people put something into boxes that travelled along the conveyor belt into the distance. I looked closer and was shocked to see that human babies were being put into the boxes on the conveyor belt and sent off to war. This supervisor person caught a glimpse of me and demanded that I start packing the babies into boxes, but I refused.

The next thing I knew, I was in a half destroyed building. The roof had gone and there was rubble all around me. I was with some other people and we were given weapons, guns, ammunition and gear. The wall in front of me caved in leaving an open space through which to climb. Immediately I knew what my mission was... to rescue the babies.

Did you know that you were born into a battlefield? Of course there are wars all over the world and to live with the daily threat of danger must be a terrifying experience. The war that I'm talking about is an unseen war where there is a battle over your soul. The dream contained picture language to communicate a spiritual concept. Like those babies, the moment you come into this world there is an enemy with evil intent, looking to send you out in your teenage years unprepared and vulnerable.

The enemy uses people like those at the conveyor belt to carry out his plans. Some are bad role models, using bad language and false lifestyles to fool millions, who follow them like sheep. Many take it all on board unaware their lives are being influenced in negative ways. We have been born into this; a battlefield where the default worldview is anti-God. It can be a tough environment to grow up in. Access to harmful content is freely available further damaging the vulnerable. Those with faith are often teased and in its place ungodly mind-sets are force-fed through the media and online. It's a battlefield where the truth is deliberately drowned out and where constant attempts to discredit faith are waged.

Put it like that and it's easy to understand the words of David concerning those who speak of God with evil intent, who misuse His name and who rebel against God. Hate here is an intentionally strong term because the innocent are being harmed by the actions of the wicked. In a battle where it's truth verses lies, following the right one will make all the difference.

God wants you to know the truth, as it will set you free from things that will try to hold back your potential. God wants you to know who you are in Him, so that you won't be tempted to be someone else. That will only lead to a false and unhappy life, when there is a life to the full just waiting for you to enjoy.

Every person has a choice as to what part they will play in this battle. Is it for good or for evil? Are you going to fight and rescue those in need, or will you go with the flow and miss out on the reason for being here? You have a role to fulfil in this battle. It's expected that like Jesus you will be attacked, accused and rejected. Will you follow in His footsteps bringing heaven to earth and proclaiming freedom for the captives?

HAVING A CLEAR OUT

#Day37

"Search me, O God, and know my heart;"   (Psalm 139:23)

Imagine it's the summer holidays. It's raining outside so you're planning on a pyjama day, playing on the games console and generally being a bit lazy. Then your mum comes in and says the words no one wants to hear, "We're having a bit of a clear out today." Suddenly going outside in the rain doesn't sound so bad!

After first tidying your room for floor space, I wonder where you would start? Perhaps the wardrobe would be first on the list? I expect working out which clothes you can't fit into might begin to create a pile for the charity shop. Then there are things stuffed into drawers. As you continue your search you begin to unearth items that have been hidden from view for ages. This is the start of a pile of things for the bin; socks with holes in, empty deodorant bottles and out of date food! Then your mum comes in and begins to suggest other items she believes should also find a new home and a difference of opinion occurs!

All of this searching unearths unwanted things that have been taking up space, which have restricted your use of your room and wardrobe. We read the words, *"Search me, O God, and know my heart,"* where the writer is actively inviting God to help him have a clear out inside his own heart. It's like he is giving God the key to his heart, to deal with things that are holding the Psalmist back.

As this process begins the question might come to mind "What happens if God finds something in my life that I don't want Him to focus on?" Could it be that God might show me an activity I've been enjoying that I didn't even realise was wrong? As soon as God highlights an issue, we are faced with the challenge of what to do next. It could be anything from watching a particular TV show, wasting precious commodities like time, or the way we treat certain individuals. All of these things (and more) we might do without thinking. Yet as God searches our lives and brings items to our attention, do we go "Oh. Do I really want to change that?" So inviting God to search our heart may be a bigger thing to ask God than we first realised; yet it's an important step in following Jesus and going deeper with Him.

Another challenge that asking God to search your heart might bring is, what happens if God wants to work on something in me that I want Him to leave alone? If God needs to work on a bad attitude that you or I have, He may need to lead us through some trials in order to shape us. Some things are such that just pointing them out for us to deal with isn't enough. Sometimes we need to go through an experience so we come out as stronger and better people. Could it be that God wants you to talk to someone you are having a feud with and agree terms of peace or even to apologise? Things like this or admitting to telling a lie (if you have actually told one!) are hard to do, but are necessary as God works within your heart.

To ask God to search your heart, without being willing to change your ways is like going through your wardrobe, finding unwanted bits, rubbish and stuff that is too small and putting it all back in afterwards. Being a true disciple of Jesus is all about discovering what pleases the heart of God and submitting to His ways. If you are willing to let God change you, He will thoroughly transform your life and shape you into your true identity. It may not be an easy process at times, but the things of most value are the hardest to come by.

Change my heart O God!!! I give You full access to see those things within that You want to work on. I want You to make me more like You. I want to be known as Yours and I realise that it is worth giving things up that might stand in the way. Whatever the process and however the outcome, please search my heart and make me more like You. In Jesus' name!

READY TO BE TESTED

#Day38

"test me and know my anxious thoughts."   (Psalm 139:23)

There are two types of tests that come along in life; those we are prepared for and those we aren't. Take for example your school exams. Most of the time you get a fair amount of warning that an exam is coming up. You know the subject and hopefully you will have been taught on it during lesson times! Before the event you are told the date and time of your exam and it's wise to study what you've learned in case any of it has fallen out of your brain. Then when the day arrives, you have your pencil sharpened (or pen) plus a spare and you go into that exam room ready to be tested. These sorts of tests are purely focused on academic ability, answering questions or creating something written or hand made.

The other type of test is the one that you'll be less prepared for; because you'll be tested on things that you can't study for. I'm talking about a test of character – what inner strength you have. So if you wanted to join the SAS (Special Air Service) they wouldn't just train you to be good at unarmed combat and shooting weapons. No, they'll also be looking to see if you are a good team member, that you can survive in harsh environments and withstand tough interrogation. What they are looking for is something that has developed inside a person through experience and hardship, where facts learned or skills developed don't quite cut it.

In order to discover whether recruits have the character to make it in the SAS they are subjected to random tests. It might be at 2am rookies are woken up and taken to a remote location and given a challenge to complete. Will all of the recruits give their best or will any let their team down at a key moment when tiredness gets the better of them? It's in times of weakness that the strength of our character is made known.

It's unlikely that God will want to test you on whether you know the order of the books of the Bible, but He will want to see how much of His word you have put into practice. How deliberately have you surrendered to Him in the way you live your life, sacrificing your wants in place of God's desires for your life? Often it's the choices we make which determine the shape and strength of our character. Without fully realising it, we can prioritise the wrong things. An athlete has to make the choice between doing something they want, like having parties and enjoying cream cakes, or sacrificing those things to spend time in training and eating well.

Good character is often developed through sacrifice. Time is precious. We only have about 16 waking hours each day. Much of the day is spent at school, waiting for stuff, eating and other things which we don't have much choice about. The way we spend the time we have left will impact on how our character develops. The person who spends 8 hours a day watching TV will turn out differently from the one who devotes their time to serving others. The experiences they have will be vastly different. The one who is out helping others will be experiencing real life, encountering hardship and developing some important life skills. Which one will be more able to cope when they are away at Uni with no money in the bank?

We read the words *"test me, and know my anxious thoughts."* The idea of this word *"anxious"* here refers to ways that put something else in the place of God. Do you turn to anger in times of stress, or is that something you used to do, but have learned to overcome with self-control? Good character refuses to be controlled, aware of the negative outcome on yourself and others when giving in to rage.

Every one of us will have different weaknesses that will need testing in different ways. Inviting God to test you is a good thing when you are willing to be changed. God can do a lot with a person who asks God to show them where they have put Him in second place. You become the best version of you when you put God first.

Father God. I give you permission to search me and test me. I know that when you test my character, it is for my good! In Jesus name!

REVIVING THE SOUL

#Day39

"See if there is any offensive way in me,"　　　　(Psalm 139:24)

I have to tell you the incredible story of something that happened in Coleraine, Northern Ireland in 1859. During a class at school, a boy suddenly became so aware that He was far away from God, convinced of how terrible his own sin was; that he was not able to work! His teacher sent him home with a boy who was a Christian. As they made their way home, the boy was so unhappy that when passing an empty house they went in to pray. The boy then gave his life to Jesus and suddenly felt changed. Immediately he returned to school to tell his teacher "I am so happy: I have the Lord Jesus in my heart!" This innocent testimony had its effect on the class, as boy after boy went outside. The head master, who looked out of the window to see what was going on, saw the boys dotted around the school yard each kneeling in prayer. So overcome was the head master that he sent the boy out to comfort the other boys.

The report says "Soon the whole school was in a strange disorder, and the ministers sent for remained all day dealing with seekers after peace— schoolboys, schoolgirls, teachers, parents and friends, the premises being thus occupied till eleven o'clock at night. These happenings stirred the whole district." [a]

What a powerful occurrence!! From time to time God will work in an especially obvious way, where whole communities experience unusual happenings such as these. Christians call such surprising happenings "revival," which is a term that refers to a set of ongoing supernatural acts of God over a set period of time. [b] People talk about feeling aware of God's presence being so close, almost like you could touch Him. You can read about the first such revival in the Bible from Acts chapter 2 onwards.

Almost every time God works in this way, people become suddenly aware of how terrible sin is, as well as how real God is. It's like God becomes so evidently close, that the truth about where we stand before God is very obvious. What follows next is an inner conflict where people realise their desperate need to make peace with God. This happened so powerfully in Wales in 1904 where whole communities were transformed. Judges in the local court houses had days where there were no cases of criminal activity to hear, because the crime rate had fallen so drastically as God made Himself real to people.

I haven't yet experienced revival, although I remember when I gave my life to Jesus as a boy. I was sitting in church and as my dad preached I realised that I hadn't made my peace with God. I don't know who noticed, but I felt like the whole world was caving in on me! I wrestled with leaving it 'til later, but I just couldn't leave it. God was pressing in on my heart.

In this world it's easy to mistakenly think that the wrong things we do don't matter. We see people getting away with worse crimes than ours without justice and we think "I'm not doing too badly." Yet actually when God highlights *"any offensive ways"* in us, it can be a powerful experience where an inner conflict ensues. Suddenly we realise those things that to us seemed quite small were actually huge and we want to flee from God under the intensity of the conviction of it.

We find our identity in God as forgiven children of God. I'm talking totally forgiven!! Not like when someone says you are forgiven, but then brings it up again the next time you do something wrong. When God forgives, all condemnation is removed. So when God highlights our wrongdoings to us, it's not to make us feel bad about ourselves; but rather so we can enjoy our identity as forgiven people with our sin removed!

Father God. I feel very vulnerable when I admit to the things that I have done wrong. I realise that You know the things that I have done and that they are not a surprise to You. Thank You Jesus that You gave Your life for me so that I could have peace with God. Please show me my offensive ways, so that I can allow You to cleanse me and change me!

PRAYER SPACE

Take this time to talk to God and to think deeply about some questions about where you stand before God.

Father God. I ask You to search my heart. Please reveal to me what you find.

1) Do I allow You to have space in my rest times?

(How do I let God into those times?)

2) Do I invite You to help me in my work times?

(When and where do I do this?)

3) Do I seek You or flee from You?

4) Do I try to hide from you when I'm tempted to go and do dark things?

5) Do I recognise Your work in my life?

6) Do I thank You for the way You have made me?

7) Do I trust You with my future?

(How do I do this?)

8) Do I value Your words by paying close attention to them?

9) Do I really want to know You?

(When have I set time aside to do this recently?)

10) Search me O God!! Where do I place other things ahead of You?

(What things do I place higher than You God?)

GOD'S EVERLASTING WAY

#Day40

"Search me, O God, and know my heart; test me and know my anxious thoughts. See if there is any offensive way in me, and lead me in the way everlasting. " (Psalm 139:23-24)

Years ago, my friend Matt and I wanted to take in a bit of culture. So we thought we'd go to see one of those historical period dramas at our local cinema. Previously we'd been to see movies with more action in them, but this was a first for me. The film *Sense and Sensibility* was on, and being the afternoon we didn't expect it to be that well attended. As we entered the cinema and sat down, we realised that this particular film was very popular with women, all a lot older than us.

As the lights dimmed and with minutes to go before the start of the film, Matt says to me "Shall I do the 'Yeah' thing when it starts?" I'm like, "the 'yeah' thing??" I have to tell you at this point that Matt likes to get psyched up for a film. Normally this goes down well in a big movie theatre, where at the start of an action movie he would yell out "YEAH!!!" and everybody is like "this is gonna be amazing!" Unfortunately our Jane Austen film wasn't in the action movie genre and the audience watching weren't the type to get super excited about an opening title. So my reply to Matt was, "umm… not really." Well Matt was very much into the idea, so I said "Oh go on then." I think Matt thought that I was also going to yell, but I had absolutely no intention of doing that.

As the opening credits appeared, Matt took a deep breath and yelled "YEAH!!!!!" in an incredibly loud voice. I have never seen anyone jump as high as those ladies sitting in front of us did on that day. Suddenly everyone was looking at us (in the dark – thankfully). The usher came running down the aisle and shining a torch at us, asked what was going on.

Matt replied as innocently as you like "I'm just excited that the film is about to start."

Are you excited about starting everlasting life? A lot of people see God's everlasting way being all about going to heaven. Maybe because you are young and with all your life ahead of you, this event seems a wee bit far off? Well I have exciting news for you! You don't have to wait for death to start enjoying eternity! For those who follow Jesus, eternity has already started here on earth! The phrase *"lead me in the way everlasting,"* talks about events that occur in our lives that stretch far into the distant future, but definitely refers to life on earth as a starting point.

Has eternity started for you? Have you decided to follow Jesus? Maybe you have put off making that choice to another time. Some people are afraid of losing the freedom to do what they want, but actually we are made free when we come to Jesus. Those in Christ Jesus have access to God's power that makes us free from the control of negative influences like sin and fear. When those things come to pull us down, we can find the strength to fight back in a way that we never had before. As God leads us in His ways, we can enjoy His personal presence with us as He guides, protects and provides for us. God leads us into freedom. Searching for your identity through things that go against God's everlasting way will lead to disappointment and confusion. Your Maker knows you better than anyone! You are not a mistake! He has a way for you that is joyful and free; not weighed down by lies or fakery. God knows the genuine you. Just like my mate Matt, God is excited about your life as it starts along His everlasting way. It's like God is going "YEAH!!!!"

When He was on earth Jesus told His disciples to tell people that the kingdom of heaven was at hand. Part of your purpose is to bring heaven's everlasting ways to here on earth. That's why prayer is such a powerful weapon. So use it often!

As we end our 40 day journey through Psalm 139 you have a lot to be excited about. There is a wealth of potential that God has built into you. Much of it may be sleeping, ready to be awakened at the right moment.

Some of it will occur as your body grows and develops. So this is not the time to decide who you are going to be for the rest of your life! God knows what that will be. Give Him your life and allow Him to search your heart, drawing out your potential as He stays close by through it all.

He will have ideas that you never thought of, as well as the means to make it all happen. He made you wonderful!

FATHER GOD, investigate my life;
get all the facts first-hand.
I'm an open book to You;
even from a distance, You know what I'm thinking.
You know when I leave and when I get back;
I'm never out of Your sight.
You know everything I'm going to say
before I start the first sentence.

I look behind me and You're there,
then up ahead and You're there, too—
Your reassuring presence, coming and going.
This is too much, too wonderful—
I can't take it all in!

Is there any place I can go to avoid Your Spirit?
to be out of Your sight?
If I climb to the sky, You're there!
If I go underground, You're there!
If I flew on morning's wings
to the far western horizon,
You'd find me in a minute—
You're already there waiting!
Then I said to myself, "Oh, he even sees me in the dark!
At night I'm immersed in the light!"
It's a fact: darkness isn't dark to You;
night and day, darkness and light, they're all the same to You.

Oh yes, You shaped me first inside, then out;
You formed me in my mother's womb.
I thank You, High God—You're breath taking!
Body and soul, I am marvellously made!
I worship in adoration—what a creation!
You know me inside and out,
You know every bone in my body;
You know exactly how I was made, bit by bit,
how I was sculpted from nothing into something.
Like an open book, You watched me grow from conception to birth;
all the stages of my life were spread out before You,
The days of my life all prepared
before I'd even lived one day.

Your thoughts—how rare, how beautiful!
God, I'll never comprehend them!
I couldn't even begin to count them—
any more than I could count the sand of the sea.
Oh, let me rise in the morning and live always with You!

And please, God, do away with wickedness for good!
And you murderers—out of here!—
all the men and women who belittle You, God,
infatuated with cheap god-imitations.
See how I hate those who hate You, GOD,
see how I loathe all this godless arrogance;
I hate it with pure, unadulterated hatred.
Your enemies are my enemies!

Investigate my life, O God,
find out everything about me;
Cross-examine and test me,
get a clear picture of what I'm about;
See for Yourself whether I've done anything wrong—
then guide me on the road to eternal life [a]

THE MESSAGE

PRAYER SPACE

If you would like to take God up on His invitation to know Him, you can do this by praying this prayer to Him. If you can speak (or whisper) it, all the better!

Thank You Jesus for Your invitation.

I come just as I am.

I know I have done many things wrong.

I thank You for dying on the cross for me.

Cleanse my life.

Set me free from the past.

I open the door of my life now.

I receive Your invitation.

I receive You into my life.

Come in by Your Holy Spirit.

Fill me with Your peace, Your presence, Your power.

Help me to build my life on You

Thank You Jesus for hearing my prayer.

PRAYER SPACE

You are now a follower of Jesus and part of God's family!!! Why not draw, write, doodle or scribble down anything that you want to say to God…

END NOTES

#Day19

a "Don't you worry child," Swedish House Mafia © Sony/ATV Music publishing LLC, Universal Music Publishing Group, Kobalt Music Publishing Ltd

#Day 21

a Scripture taken from NEW AMERICAN STANDARD BIBLE©, Copyright © 1960, 1962, 1963, 1968, 1971, 1972, 1973, 1975, 1977, 1995 by The Lockman Foundation. Used by permission

#Day26

a As of the time of writing an app for this can be found on Google Play called "Binary Talk."

#Day39

a J. Edwin Orr "The Fervent Prayer: The worldwide impact of the Great Awakening of 1858." Moody Press, Chicago. Also W. Arthur, "The revival in Ballymena and Coleraine, pp. 12ff

b For further reading on Revival:
I saw the Welsh Revival – David Matthews
Like a mighty wind – Mel Tari
True stories of the miracles of Azusa Street and Beyond – Tommy Welchel
Revival in the Hebrides – Duncan Campbell
J. Edwin Orr – Can God?

#Day40

a The Message Bible. Unless otherwise indicated, all Scripture quotations are taken from *THE MESSAGE*, copyright © 1993, 2002, 2018 by Eugene H. Peterson. Used by permission of NavPress. All rights reserved. Represented by Tyndale House Publishers, Inc

NOTES

NOTES

NOTES

NOTES

Like or follow us on

...to hear about previews, freebies and new publications from the Inspire series.

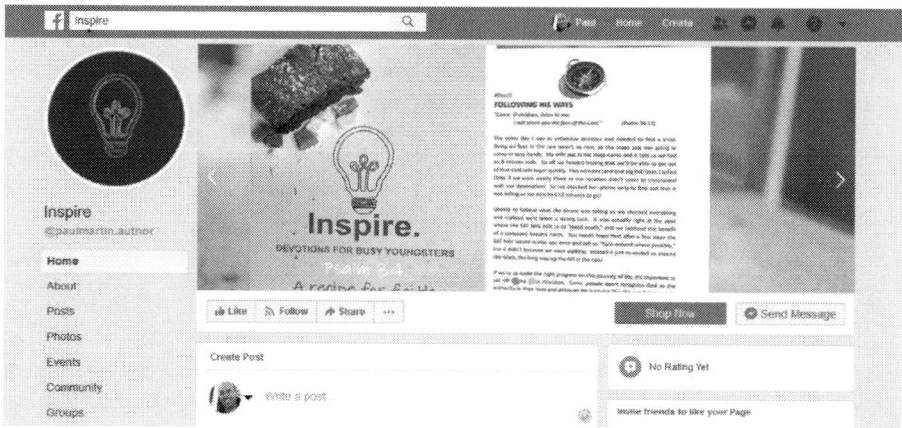

Available now at Amazon.

A *Recipe for faith* is a 40 day devotional for young people and teenagers. This book deals with issues of worry, anxiety and fear from the perspective of David found in Psalm 34. Could you imagine being on the run from the King and his army? In your quest for refuge you flee to the most unlikely place in a desperate attempt to find safety. You're afraid, very afraid. Once this fearful moment has passed, God speaks and you write this Psalm.

Psalm 34 will be an incredible encouragement to you as you find your way through the ups and downs of life. It's in the busyness of everyday life that God wants to talk to us; where we're battling fear or when life is stretching us beyond our ability to cope. This devotional is written so that you will discover a fresh connection with Father God. By digging deep into His words we are going to be inspired with God's perspective on those negative fears that don't do us any good. He wants to lead us into a place of faith, so that we will know what to do when fear comes knocking. Hopefully you'll see this as a chat between friends, looking at our lives, having a laugh and gaining strength for the fight. Why not join me in conversation? Otherwise I'll just be talking to myself!

Over the page is one of the devotions from the book...

THE FEAR OF THE LORD

"Oh, fear the Lord, you His saints,"   (Psalm 34:9)

Imagine you are at home one day and you hear a knock at the door. You get to the door and a basket has been left on your doorstep. As you look at the basket you can see it is well padded and looks like a cosy home for something to snuggle in. You look to see if anyone is around, but they are long gone. So you take a peek inside the basket. To your surprise there's a wee kitten inside! The kitten looks up at you with its big eyes and squeaks.

Well there's nothing to be done but to bring it inside. After a quick search on the internet you discover it needs special milk and a feeding bottle, which you manage to source. Watching the kitten enjoying his first feed with you is a special moment and you decide to keep him.

However after a week or so you slowly begin to realise something about this kitten... that "kitten" is the wrong word for it. A more accurate term would be "cub." Yes this is no domesticated cat; you have taken in a lion! Of course lions require a whole other level of taking care of than a simple house cat. Apart from the size issues and visits you would need to the butchers for feeding time, a lion requires a certain amount of respect that you don't need to give to your common cat. For a start there are safety issues. You may have a bond with the lion which means he may never attack you, but I expect most visitors would not be viewed by the lion in quite the same way. However you look at him, that lion is stronger than you and can pretty much do his own thing if he wants to.

As we've seen, the word "fear" can have a number of meanings. It can be a healthy awareness of danger (such as being in the vicinity of an erupting volcano); but it can also be an unhealthy anxiety of the unknown.

So what does it mean to fear God? It's a bit like our lion scenario. The nature of a lion is that it is strong, powerful and if you have ever heard one roar at close range, your heart will beat much, much, faster! So we give the lion the respect he deserves! To approach a lion without the respect fitting a lion is a very unwise move. Imagine if someone were to give the lion a kick up the bum like some would mistreat a domestic cat; they would be fortunate if they escaped the house with all their limbs!

So when it says *"Oh, fear the Lord, you His saints"* it refers to a healthy respect for who God is. He is the Almighty, our creator. He knows His own mind and as we read in the previous verse, He is only good. Is He safe? Like the lion, He is not safe. So we do well to be on His side! God is love; but He is also holy. This means He is pure and cannot allow evil to get away with its plans in any way. At some point the significance of a crime against another must be brought to light and justice result. We all agree that thieves and murders must face justice. Oh and liars can't be allowed to trick people; and what about bullies who cause so much pain?

The problem is that if you really think about it, we've all done evil in some way. I'm sure you'll agree, like me you've done things wrong that have hurt others, hurt yourself or hurt God. The Bible tells us that these actions separate us from God, showing a lack of fear of Him (Romans 3:23). The good news is that God showed His love in a practical way by paying the fine for a judgement we deserve (Romans 6:23). Like a judge, God will uphold right from wrong, but with the deepest love for you and me, He did what it took to help us avoid the consequences.

Who are His saints? They are those who take up God on His offer to pay our fine. It remains outstanding and unpaid until we do something about it. This is where Jesus comes in. God became man, lived a perfect life and allowed Himself to be unjustly executed as a criminal so that the fallout of our mistakes would be erased. I'd much rather experience God's love than His judgement! If you haven't already accepted His gift, He wants you to take it. That is why He let them put Him on a cross like a common criminal. Over the page is a prayer space to help you to take time to make the most important decision of your life. Why not take a look?

For Leaders:
Available now at Amazon.

Some youth groups have enjoyed journeying together as a group through the Psalm 34 devotional. This leader's guide contains the daily devotionals, plus 7 weekly interactive Bible study sessions to lead your youth group in discussions through the Psalm.

Also available now at Amazon

INSPIRE – A resource for busy youth workers - VOLUMES 1&2

This discussional resource is written for all those involved in youth ministry. With over 60 Bible interactive study sessions in each volume it moves chronologically through the Old and New Testament. Volume 1 tackles the big stories of the Old Testament like Noah's Ark, as well ones that may be less familiar to young people such as Job, Hagar and Eliezer.

Volume 2 continues where volume 1 left off, completing the Old Testament stories before moving on to the New. This resource is ideal for those with limited preparation time, yet want to take young people deeper into God's word and understand its applications in a more meaningful way.

Amy Walters Art & Design

Christian Graphic Design Artist

FURNACE

Amy created this logo for Paul Martin's Furnace youth group in 2015.

For enquiries and commissions e-mail
amywaltersart@gmail.com

22834411R00072

Printed in Great Britain
by Amazon